WOOD

TECHNOLOGY AND PROCESSES

Instructor's Resource Guide

Keyed to the 1994 edition of the textbook *Wood Technology and Processes*

JOHN L. FEIRER

GLENCOE

Macmillan/McGraw-Hill

New York, New York
Columbus, Ohio
Mission Hills, California
Peoria, Illinois

Send all inquiries to:
GLENCOE DIVISION
Macmillan/McGraw-Hill
3008 W. Willow Knolls Drive
Peoria, IL 61614

ISBN 0-02-677611-1 (Instructor's Resource Guide)
ISBN 0-02-677610-3 (Text)
ISBN 0-02-677612-X (Student Workbook)

Printed in the United States of America

1 2 3 4 5 6 7 8 9 10   VER   97 96 95 94 93

Table of Contents

Preface

This guide contains practical suggestions for using the textbook *Wood Technology and Processes* and the accompanying *Student Workbook.* Classroom experiences with this text provided the basis for the guide's content. Teachers should therefore find the guide helpful for planning and teaching a course of study in their own classrooms and laboratories.

USING THE TEXTBOOK

Wood Technology and Processes is a comprehensive woodworking text that includes coverage of technology, materials, tools, machines, and methods. Section I discusses woodworking technology, safety, and careers. Sections II, III, and IV discuss the basics of hand woodworking. Section V discusses the use of fundamental machines in woodworking. Section VI deals with wood science. Section VII discusses manufacturing, construction, communication, and transportation systems and their relationship to woodworking. Section VIII consists of projects.

The text matter in *Wood Technology and Processes* is accompanied by many photographs and drawings. Second color has been used to emphasize certain parts or procedures and to add visual appeal. Full-color inserts have been included to show the true beauty of the various woods.

Most teachers give reading assignments on a regular basis. A major problem for the teacher is the varied reading skills of the students in the class. There will always be some students who will be able to handle the reading assignments without difficulty. Other students may have some reading problems, while still others are actually nonreaders.

Students with reading difficulties and students who are nonreaders can still make good use of a textbook by utilizing the illustrations. Verbal instruction using the photographs and line drawings can be helpful to all students.

A major concern in selecting a textbook is to be certain of the reading level. *Wood Technology and Processes* was written with vocabulary and sentence structure based on the reading abilities of beginning industrial technology students. Words, sentences, and paragraphs were designed to make the reading easy and to increase interest, understanding, and effective study.

USING THE STUDENT WORKBOOK

The *Wood Technology and Processes Student Workbook* is an aid to getting students to use their textbooks properly. It helps students learn to read and to follow directions. The unit reviews can be used as outside assignments or as in-class assignments following demonstrations and lectures. Questions from the workbook can also be used for short tests. The Science and Math activities can be used for remediation or to extend learning to include other disciplines.

USING THE INSTRUCTOR'S RESOURCE GUIDE

The *Wood Technology and Processes Instructor's Resource Guide* contains material to help you organize, present, and evaluate your teaching program. Several factors will influence how much of this guide you might use in your program, including:

- Length of the course. The number of units covered and the time that can be devoted to project activities will depend on how many weeks are available.
- Number and kind of students. The size of the class and the age of the students will affect the amount of material that can be used. Also, special plans may be needed for some groups, such as students with learning difficulties or handicaps.
- The size of the facility and the kinds and number of tools and machines available.
- The level of the course.
- The size and kind of projects.
- The amount of money students can spend on materials.

This guide includes material for use in course development ("Planning the Course"). It presents general course objectives, specific behavioral objectives, and curriculum materials.

Most school systems are continuing to emphasize *competency-based* education, particularly in technology education. Competency-based education means that the school can demonstrate with facts and figures what the students know and are able to do. The competencies to be taught are often written as *behavioral objectives.* The behavioral objectives can be written in several different formats; those presented in this guide are meant to serve as examples. You may wish to select some for your course, or you may develop a different set.

As another aid to planning the course, 9-, 18-, and 36-week course outlines and other curriculum materials have been included. Because individual courses differ greatly, there is no way this guide could provide outlines that would be suitable for every teaching situation. The curriculum materials presented here are meant to serve as guidelines only. They suggest a format for developing outlines suited to individual course needs.

This guide also contains material for use in teaching the course ("Teaching Suggestions"), including student handouts, materials on problem-solving and critical thinking, tips for using visual masters and other aids, a progress chart, and other useful information.

Planning the Course

Course planning should begin with a review of the overall goals or objectives of the course. The following is a list of course objectives for a woodworking program.

THE WOODWORKING PROGRAM: COURSE OBJECTIVES

- To develop in each student a measure of skill in the use of common tools and machines.
- To provide general all-around technical knowledge and skills.
- To discover and to develop creative technical talents in students.
- To develop worthy leisure-time interests.
- To develop problem-solving skills relating to materials and processes.
- To develop an understanding of our technical culture.
- To help students make informed educational and occupational choices.
- To develop consumer knowledge and appreciation and use of industrial products.
- To provide prevocational experience of an intensified nature for those students interested in technical work.
- To provide vocational training for students who would not otherwise have this opportunity.
- To develop an understanding of the nature and characteristics of technology.
- To develop an understanding and appreciation of science and math.

BEHAVIORAL OBJECTIVES

The use of behavioral objectives in developing a program of instruction has become widespread. Many school systems now require them. A list of behavioral objectives for woodworking is included here on pages 7–9. These can be used by the teacher in planning the course outline.

Unlike the broad statements in the course objectives, these behavioral objectives deal with specific competencies that can be measured. Each behavioral objective contains a statement of behavior that tells exactly what the student will be expected to do (the *performance*). Concrete terms such as *select, measure, sketch, build, assemble, explain, list, identify,* and *complete* are used to state these behavioral objectives.

The list of objectives also states the *conditions* under which the objectives are to be achieved; i.e.,

the equipment and materials required for carrying out the stated performance.

The *criteria* used to assess a successful performance should also be included in a behavioral objective. The criteria state the measure of acceptable performance.

CURRICULUM MATERIALS

The method of organizing curriculum materials for a course using this book can vary widely. One method is to list learning activities, technical information, and resources. Following is a list of learning activities, a list of technical information needed for carrying out learning activities, and an example of how these are combined for a typical course outline.

Learning Activities

Hand (Select from the following)
1. Read a working drawing
2. Make out a bill of materials
3. Plan the procedure in doing jobs
4. Check material when received
5. Measure and divide spaces with a rule
6. Lay out a pattern on stock
7. Check the layout
8. Lay out curves with dividers or compass
9. Divide spaces with dividers
10. Gauge with a pencil
11. Gauge with a marking gauge
12. Test for squareness with the try square
13. Lay out square cuts with the try square
14. Adjust a jack plane or a smooth plane
15. Plane a surface true
16. Plane an edge square with an adjoining surface
17. Plane end grain
18. Proceed properly in squaring up a board
19. Saw to a line with a crosscut saw or ripsaw
20. Saw to a line with a back saw
21. Saw inside or outside curves with a coping saw
22. Round edges
23. Finish outside curves
24. Finish inside curves
25. Drill holes in wood
26. Countersink holes
27. Bore holes with an auger bit
28. Fasten with screws
29. Trim or pare with a chisel

(List continued on pages 9–12.)

Conditions	Performance	Criteria
1. Given a 12-inch scale and a 300 mm scale,	the student will identify ten described increments on each scale	with a success of 70% on each scale.
2. Given a 12-inch rule and a 300 mm rule and 10 measurable objects,	the student will measure 10 objects	so well that $7/10$ are measured to the nearest $1/16''$ or 1 mm.
3. Given unit cost and number of units for 10 problems,	the student will calculate the cost of materials	for $7/10$ of the problems correctly.
4. Given project assignments and measuring equipment,	the student will add, subtract, divide, and multiply	as necessary to design, lay out, and assemble project.
5. Given a drawing assignment,	the student will add, subtract, divide, and multiply	as necessary to center and lay out the drawing assignment.
6. Given a list of glossary terms,	the student will (1) write or (2) match the correct definition	with an accuracy of 70%.
7. Given symbols or abbreviations representative of subject area,	the student will identify them	with an accuracy of 70%.
8. Given a reading assignment related to subject matter,	the student will identify important points of the assignment	and list them according to teacher/ student established criteria.
9. Given a study guide and a textbook,	the student will complete the study guide	with an accuracy of 80%.
10. Given a list of terms appropriate to area,	the student will spell the terms	with an accuracy of 70%.
11. Given a plan sheet and choice of projects,	the student will complete the planning sheet	to teacher/student established criteria.
12. Given a choice of industry-related topics,	the student will give oral presentation to class	according to teacher/student established criteria.
13. Given a list of careers,	the student will identify individual interests	by writing a career report of choice.
14. Given a list of occupational and leisure time activities,	the student will identify those that are primarily leisure time and those that are occupational	with 70% accuracy.
15. Given appropriate time and materials for careers,	the student will describe which industry-related or career areas interest the student most	and list three reasons why.
16. After having completed any product,	the student will verbally or by a brief report tell what was gained in the experience and how, if given a second chance, he/she would improve his/her work	so that the student recognizes any strengths and weaknesses and how to improve.

Conditions	Performance	Criteria
17. Given a variety of completed projects,	the student will determine and list those items which create pride in work	so the student will be able to relate this to his/her own work.
18. Given a list of positive and negative industrial social behaviors,	the student will distinguish between them	and explain the rationale for the choices.
19. Given information on how well he/she does on specific skills,	the student will identify those which he/she thinks require further development and improvement	and will identify a minimum of three areas.
20. Given the design and plan sheet,	the student will design and complete plan sheet for a project	and have plan sheet checked out and okayed.
21. Given a mass production project and use of equipment,	the student will participate in the development and production of a product	according to teacher/student established criteria.
22. Given a project assignment and available tools and equipment,	the student will design, plan, and construct a project	according to teacher/student established criteria.
23. Given various tools and equipment,	the student will maintain and care for tools and equipment	according to teacher/student established criteria.
24. Given a list of ten wood materials,	the student will identify the industries that are involved in processing the materials	with 70% accuracy.
25. Given a display of hand tools,	the student will identify them	with 70% accuracy.
26. After having been shown a variety of different power hand tools,	the student will visually identify them	with 70% accuracy.
27. Given the appropriate drawing, templates, instruction, drawing equipment and materials,	the student will lay out the size and shape of a project	so that it is within $1/16$ inch [1.5 mm] of drawing dimensions.
28. Given materials for shop skills such as driving nails, pulling nails, sawing, filing, abrading, polishing, chiseling, etc.,	the student will demonstrate the correct usage of tools	according to safe practices.
29. Given assorted mechanical fasteners,	the student will be able to explain correct usage	and pass written test with 70% accuracy.
30. Given a list of abrasive materials,	the student will identify them	and pass written test with 70% accuracy.
31. Given necessary upholstery materials,	the student will complete a pad seat	to teacher/student approval.
32. Given abrasive materials,	the student will follow proper abrading techniques	with final scratch marks even and uniform.

Conditions	Performance	Criteria
33. Given a display of twenty-five different woodworking hand tools,	the student will identify and write their correct names	with 70% accuracy.
34. Given the following portable electric tools: electric drill, belt sander, finishing sander, router, sabre saw, and jig saw,	the student will identify	five out of six correctly.
35. Given the following woodworking machines: radial-arm saw, jointer, planer, and table saw,	the student will identify machine adjustments, uses, and safety	and pass written test for each machine with 70% accuracy.
36. Given a list of lumber processing steps,	the student will identify and explain each	and pass written test with 70% accuracy.
37. Given the following building materials: solid lumber, plywood, veneer, hardboard, particle board, and plastic laminates,	the student will identify and explain use of each	and pass written test for each material with 70% accuracy.
38. Given twelve wood samples,	the student will identify deciduous or coniferous samples	and identify ten out of twelve correctly.
39. Given the following wood joints: butt, dado, miter, dowel, lap, rabbet, mortise-and-tenon,	the student will identify them	and pass written test with 70% accuracy.
40. Given the seven basic finishing steps: bleaching, paste wood filler, stain, sealer, finished coats, rubbing down, and waxing,	the student will describe them	and pass written test with 70% accuracy.
41. Given the following finishing methods: brushing, wiping, and spraying,	the student will describe them	and pass written test with 70% accuracy.

30. Smooth a surface with abrasives
31. Shape ends, edges, and curves with a wood file
32. Drive and draw nails
33. Set a nail or brad
34. Lay out and test bevel cuts with a sliding T bevel
35. Round or form work with a spokeshave
36. Lay out an octagon
37. Lay out and cut a chamfer
38. Hold stock with handscrews and clamps
39. Apply stain
40. Clean and care for stain brushes
41. Apply stain for two-tone effect
42. Apply fillers
43. Apply shellac
44. Clean and care for shellac brushes
45. Apply wax
46. Apply enamel
47. Clean and care for brushes
48. Transfer a design
49. Lay out an irregular design by means of squares
50. Make a butt joint
51. Sharpen edge tools, such as knives, chisels, and plane bits
52. Keep tools free from rust
53. Adjust a block plane
54. Cut curves with a compass saw
55. Do gouge work
56. Smooth a surface with a scraper

57. Lay out a hexagon
58. Prepare adhesives
59. Glue up work
60. Apply paint with brush
61. Lay out duplicate parts
62. Make a half-lap joint
63. Lay out and cut a dado joint
64. Cut a groove or a rabbet
65. Lay out and cut a cross-lap joint
66. Make an edge-to-edge glue joint
67. Lay out and cut tapers
68. Do upholstering that involves simple padding
69. Dress a screwdriver
70. Set and use an expansive bit
71. Cut curves with a turning saw
72. Lay out an ellipse
73. Put on locks
74. Put on drawer pulls
75. Fit hinges
76. Apply varnish
77. Apply lacquer
78. Apply finish with a spray gun
79. Lay out and cut a miter joint
80. Make a dowel joint
81. Lay out and cut a mortise-and-tenon joint
82. Construct a panel
83. Make a splined joint
84. Make a drawer slide
85. Make and fit a drawer
86. Fasten on a tabletop
87. Sharpen a scraper
88. Sharpen auger bits
89. Use a Forstner bit
90. Clean and care for a spray gun

Machine

Surfacer
  1. Learn the rules for safe operation and know the range of work that may be done
  2. Care for and adjust a surfacer
  3. Adjust for depth of cut
  4. Adjust and control feed
  5. Feed work into the machine

Circular Saw
  1. Learn the rules for safe operation and know the range of work that may be done
  2. Care for and adjust the saw
  3. Rip
  4. Cut off
  5. Cut grooves
  6. Cut dadoes
  7. Cut tenons
  8. Cut miters
  9. Cut tapers
  10. Resaw

Radial-arm Saw
  1. Learn the rules for safe operation and know the range of work that may be done
  2. Care for and adjust the saw
  3. Cross cut
  4. Rip

Band Saw
  1. Learn the rules for safe operation and know the range of work that may be done
  2. Care for and adjust the saw
  3. Saw curves
  4. Rip
  5. Cut off
  6. Cut tenons

Scroll, or Jig, Saw
  1. Learn the rules for safe operation and know the range of work that may be done
  2. Cut
  3. Do inlay or marquetry

Portable Saws
  1. Learn rules for safe operation
  2. Know range of work with cut-off saw
  3. Know range of work with sabre saw

Jointer
  1. Learn rules for safe operation and range of work that may be done
  2. Care for and adjust the machine
  3. Joint an edge
  4. Cut a chamfer or bevel
  5. Make a spring joint
  6. Surface narrow stock
  7. Cut a rabbet

Drill Press
  1. Learn rules for safe operation and range of work that may be done
  2. Care for and adjust the machine
  3. Drill
  4. Shape
  5. Rout

Sanders
  1. Learn rules for safe operation and range of work that may be done
  2. Operate belt and disc sanders
  3. Operate finish sander

Portable Router
  1. Learn rules for safe operation and range of work that may be done

2. Do freehand routing
3. Do inlaying

Lathe
1. Learn rules for safe operation and range of work that may be done
2. Adjust and care for the lathe
3. Center stock
4. Mount work between centers
5. Rough down with a gouge
6. Smooth with a skew
7. Lay off pattern on piece
8. Size with a sizing tool
9. Mark off with a skew
10. Trim with a cut-off tool
11. Cut shoulders with a skew
12. Cut tapers with a skew
13. Cut beads or convex surfaces with a skew
14. Scrape with a skew
15. Scrape with a diamond-point and scraping tool
16. Measure with outside calipers
17. Measure with inside calipers
18. Cut concave curves with a gouge
19. Mount work on a faceplate
20. Size work on a faceplate
21. Hollow out work on a faceplate or screw chuck
22. Sand stock in the lathe
23. Apply finish in the lathe

Technical Information

Wood Materials
1. Be able to identify the following kinds of lumber and any other kinds in common use: the pines, spruce, cypress, oak, walnut, birch, maple, mahogany, red cedar, hickory, gum, chestnut, poplar
2. Know the principal characteristics, the working properties, the chief uses, and the important sources of supply of each
3. The methods of cutting and milling lumber
4. The effect of moisture on wood
5. The standard dimensions of lumber and how they are classified
6. The nominal and the actual dimensions of lumber
7. How lumber is dried
8. How veneer and plywood are made, and their uses

Finishes
1. The purpose of finishes
2. The kinds of finishes in common use, such as stain, oil, wax, shellac, varnish, lacquer, enamel, paint

3. The durability of different finishes
4. The conditions or places in which various kinds of finishes may be used to advantage
5. Materials from which finishes are made

Adhesives
1. The kinds of adhesives
2. The preparation of adhesives
3. The conditions and requirements in use

Nails
1. The kinds of nails
2. The uses of different kinds
3. The sizes of nails
4. How nails are sold
5. How nails are manufactured

Screws
1. The kinds of screws
2. The uses of the different kinds
3. How the sizes and kinds of screws are indicated
4. How screws are sold

Abrasives and Steel Wool
1. The kinds of abrasives
2. The grades of abrasives
3. The principal uses of abrasives

Styles of Furniture
1. The distinguishing characteristics of different types and periods

The Manufacture of Wood Products
1. The location of important manufacturing plants
2. The division of labor in this industry
3. The use of automatic machinery

Joints
1. The types of joints, where they are used, and why

Hardware
1. The types of hinges and their uses
2. The installation of hardware

Careers
1. Kinds of jobs
2. Craft occupations

Manufacturing
1. Methods of selecting and applying acceptable designs
2. Reading and interpreting a working drawing
3. The calculation of cost of material for a project
4. The plan of procedure
5. Making templates and transferring designs to stock
6. Laying out designs on stock

7. Testing for squareness with a try square
8. Testing for a true surface with a straightedge
9. Checking layout
10. Checking measurements

11. The purposes and uses of different types of saws (crosscut, rip, etc.)
12. The purposes and uses of different types of planes (smooth, jack, jointer, etc.)

Typical Course Outline

This is for a unit on designing, planning, materials, and safety.

Learning Activities	Technical Information	Suggestions-Resources
Select a design Read a working drawing Make out a bill of materials Make a shop sketch Learn safety rules	Good design Techniques in planning work Reading drawings and sketches (view drawings, pictorials, alphabet of lines) Bill of materials (lumber and wood materials, standard sizes, specifying lumber, figuring board measure) Determining tools and material needs	General information (laboratory environment, working effectively in a group, objectives of course, safety procedures, dress requirements) Textbook (Units 1, 2, 3, 4, 5, 6, and 7) Workbook

TERM PLAN

A general plan should be structured for the activities and work of the school term. The plan ought to be based on length of the school term and the grading period. It should list demonstrations to be given, related information to be presented, and the discussions that are to be included. The following is an example:

First Week
1. Explain school and laboratory policies, including:
   a. Organization of the class
   b. Seating and bench assignments
   c. Textbook assignments
   d. Workbook assignments
   e. Clean-up assignments
   f. Locker assignments
   g. Objectives of the class

h. Accident procedures
   i. Emergency procedures for fire, tornado, etc.
2. Safety lesson and test
3. Project selection
4. Discussion of basic project, including bill of materials and plan of procedure

Second Week
1. Measuring tools: customary and metric
2. Demonstration on measuring and marking stock for cutting to size
3. How to use and select hand saws
4. How to adjust and assemble a plane
5. How to plane a surface

Typical Time Schedule
This time schedule is for a one-piece basic project, such as a pen holder, cutting board, or house numbers.

	Mon.	Tues.	Wed.	Thur.	Fri.
First Week	Laboratory policies	Assignments L-Safety	Safety test #1 L-Project selection	Reading a drawing Planning sheets	D-Measure and cut stock
Second Week	D-Use of planes	Work	L-Wood materials	Work	R-Careers
Third Week	FS-Hand tools	Work	Work	L-Abrasives	D-Nails and nailing
Fourth Week	D-Simple finishes	D-Coping saw and jig saw	Work	Work	Project due

D—Demonstration; L—Lecture; R—Related; FS—Filmstrip

DEMONSTRATIONS AND RELATED LESSONS

It is a good idea to develop a plan for each demonstration, related lesson, and audiovisual to be shown. Once completed, these will greatly simplify your teaching responsibilities.

Sample Demonstration Lesson Plan

Date: _____ Week: 8th Time Required: 45 min.
Topic: Turning on the wood lathe
Objective: To teach how to turn with stock held between centers (spindle).
Materials: Several pieces of wood (size 2 inch × 2 inch × 14 inch or 50 × 50 × 350 mm), rule, caliper, back saw, mallet, gouges, parting tool, and lathe.
Visual Aids: Samples of turned projects such as a lamp, mallet, salt and pepper shakers, and tool handles.
Motivation: 1. Illustrate projects that can be turned on a lathe.
              2. Discuss the kinds of lathes used in industry.
              3. Discuss the lathe and wood turning as a hobby.
              4. Review parts of lathe and its tools.
Procedure: 1. Cut stock to size.
              2. Locate centers on each end of wood.
              3. Drive spur center in place with a mallet. Why use a mallet instead of a hammer?
              4. Place the work in the lathe and adjust the tailstock.
              5. Adjust the tool rest and check by turning the work by hand. Emphasize safety.
              6. Demonstrate use of the gouge.
              7. Remove work from lathe.
Summary: 1. List steps in spindle turning.
              2. Check safety procedures when using the lathe.
Application: 1. Read Chapter 61 in the textbook.
              2. Complete Study Guide Unit. Collect pictures of turned projects.
Safety: 1. Lathe guard, goggles, proper clothing, removal of jewelry, machine adjustments and sharp tools.

Sample Related Lesson Plan

Date: _____ Week: 3rd Time Required: 45 min.
Topic: Wood: its growth, selection, and identification
Objective: To teach how a tree grows.
              To teach how lumber is cut from the log.
              To teach how to identify certain selected kinds of wood.
Materials: Wood identification chart.
              Sample section of a log.
              Samples of various kinds of wood.
Motivation: 1. Show section of finished wood with various grain patterns. What causes the wood to have this appearance?
              2. Pass around wood samples for examination. Ask students to try to identify woods by appearance.

Procedure:
1. Show the cross section of the log and identify its parts.
2. Have students make a drawing of cross section of the log.
3. Show sample of hardwood and softwood. Ask students to tell how to identify the differences.
4. If available, show film on lumbering.
5. Test students on the common woods they will use to make projects.

Questions:
1. Define these terms: cambium, medullary rays, hardwood, softwood.
2. Describe the methods of cutting logs into boards.
3. Explain how lumber is seasoned.
4. Describe the following woods: pine, walnut, and poplar.

Summary:
1. Review parts of a tree.
2. Give test on five or six common woods.

Assignment: Students will select stock for their project.

Reference: Chapters 2 and 66 in textbook.

Teaching Suggestions

REPRODUCIBLES

Special materials can be given to students. These are included at the end of this guide. Permission is granted by the publisher to reproduce them for classroom use. They include Handouts, Worksheets, and Transparency Masters.

USING A GLOSSARY

A glossary can be used in a variety of ways. It can help students learn to spell words, define words, and identify a word when only its definition is given.

A glossary of woodworking terms is included at the back of the textbook.

AUDIOVISUAL MATERIALS

A wide variety of audiovisual materials in the form of transparencies, transparency masters, filmstrips, and movies is available. In the following list, the first two references will help you in selecting visual aids. The rest are suppliers of visual aids.

Educators Guide to Free Films
Educators Progress Service, Inc.
Randolph, WI 53965

Index to Vocational and Technical Education
(Multimedia); First Edition
National Information Center for Educational Media
(Micem)

University of California
University Park
Los Angeles, CA 90007

Abraxas Films
Box 186
Capitola, CA 95010

AIMS Instructional Media, Inc.
626 Justin Avenue
Glendale, CA 91201

Association-Sterling Films
512 Burlington Avenue
La Grange, IL 60525

Barr Films
3490 Foothill Blvd.
Pasadena, CA 91107

Glencoe Division
Macmillan/McGraw-Hill
3008 W. Willow Knolls Drive
Peoria, IL 61614

Bergwall Productions, Inc.
839 Stewart Avenue
Garden City, NY 11530

DCA Educational Products, Inc.
424 Valley Road
Warrington, PA 18976

Greystone Films, Inc.
336 Bayview Avenue
Amityville, NY 11701

McGraw-Hill Text Films
330 W. 42nd Street
New York, NY 10036

Meridian Education Corporation
205 E. Locust St.
Bloomington, IL 61701

Modern Talking Picture Service, Inc.
3718 Broadway
Kansas City, MO 64111
or
201 South Jefferson Avenue
St. Louis, MO 63103

Prentice-Hall Media
150 White Plains Road
Tarrytown, NY 10591

RMI Media Productions, Inc.
120 West 72nd Street
Kansas City, MO 64114

Society for Visual Education, Inc.
Division: The Singer Company
1345 Diversey Parkway
Chicago, IL 60614

Stanley Tools
600 Myrtle Street
New Britain, CT 06050

3M Company
Educational Service
Box 3100
St. Paul, MN 55101

PROJECTS

Basic Project

The best method of getting a class started is to provide the students with a basic project. For this first project the teacher should supply the drawing, bill of materials, procedure, and the rough stock. A small, simple project, such as a pen and pencil holder, simple book rack, a cutting board, or house numbers, may be appropriate if this is the first experience in the wood lab. For students who have had some woodworking experience, a more advanced project, such as a serving tray, fruit tray, or letter rack, might be better. The basic project should:
- Be attractive and useful to the student.
- Have intrinsic value.
- Provide experiences with basic tools and, for more advanced students, basic machines.
- Be flexible enough to allow for some design changes.

- Be completed within a limited, specified length of time.

Individual Projects

It is easier to "sell" the student on a project that he/she can select from a group. Students may be allowed to select a project from four or five designs provided by the teacher and based on the following:
- That the same learning units will be covered in each project.
- That the work will be of about equal difficulty.
- That the student will be required to make his/her own plan from a print or model.

In addition, student interest can be held more easily if he/she is allowed to select a project from outside the group which would fit into the group requirements.

There are some disadvantages to individual projects. One is that they take more of the teacher's time than a single project that is assigned to all students. Getting out materials is also more of a problem.

Mass Production

A portion of any course should be devoted to mass producing a product. The teacher may provide the plans, jigs, and fixtures and help in the organization. The class should be organized into four major groups:
- Product engineering.
- Production planning.
- Manufacturing.
- Marketing.

Limited Equipment

Students may be divided into groups and rotated so that each group has an opportunity to use a lathe, router, jig saw, and other tools that are in limited supply.

The Metric System

At least one of the projects required should apply the metric measuring system. Students can be asked to convert one drawing from customary to metric, use a simple 300-mm scale to do the measurements and complete the project, or the teacher can supply a project designed in metric measurements.

Free Choice

Depending on the length of the course or the level of student ability, students may be allowed to choose a project based on the following considerations:

- Is it easy to correlate the project with the units in the course outline?
- Is it easy to maintain student interest?
- Is the project within the student's level of ability?
- Does it provide an opportunity for the student to make project plans?

SYSTEMS OF TECHNOLOGY

If time permits, students should be involved in some kind of learning activity in each of the areas covered in Section VII. The following are some suggestions:

- Upholstery. A small footstool might be made as an individual project or as a mass-produced project. Then each student could make a padded seat of his/her own design for the top.
- Patternmaking. A one-piece pattern can be made for a small project such as a pen holder or house numbers. The pattern could be cast in the metal shop or it could be used "as is" to complete the project.
- Manufacturing. A portion of any course should include some mass production experience. A good example of a mass-produced product is the book holder.
- Construction. If possible, a construction activity such as making a piece of outdoor furniture or a scale model of a home should be included. However, if these activities cannot be carried out, then a day or two of related study should be devoted to the construction industry. This might include a film on home construction or a demonstration of a mock-up for a section of a home to illustrate the various parts. Students might also be required to visit a home under construction and write a report.
- Communication. Communication can be covered in its relationship to a manufacturing or construction project. For example, the class can practice communication among the various "departments" involved in mass producing a project. In construction, one assignment might be to write a report on a visit to a construction site.
- Transportation. Students can design and build a conveyor system to use in mass producing a product. They could also visit a furniture store and write a report on the kinds of vehicles used in the warehouse; or they could describe the vehicles used in constructing a home.

PROGRESS CHART

A progress chart, such as appears after the Answer Keys, should be used for each class. The teacher should fill in those major items that will be used for evaluating the student, including projects, tests, outside assignments, and so forth.

TESTS AND EVALUATION

The teacher should explain to the students the basis for the final grades in the class. This might include the following:

- Projects completed—40 to 50 percent.
- Short tests—10 to 20 percent.
- Final test—20 percent.
- Class dependability, cooperation, participation, and involvement—10 percent.
- Work attitudes and habits related to safety, shop maintenance, improvements—10 percent.

The teacher may post the following chart, telling how the projects will be evaluated.

Evaluation of Projects

Planning	2	4	6	8
Procedure	Unable to work from the plan	Some steps wrong or missing	A few minor changes needed	Plan was complete; no changes needed
Drawing	Incorrectly drawn, poor dimensioning	Able to use with some changes	A few needed dimensions missing	Able to use and work from with no changes
Design & usefulness of project	Not usable for purpose intended	Able to use with some changes	No changes made; could be redesigned	Well designed for purpose intended
Problem-solving ability	Solved no problems	Solved only the easy problems	Solved nearly all the problems	Solved all the problems

Evaluation of Projects

Construction	5	10	15	20
Appearance	Assembled poorly; not cleaned up	Not very neat; good assembly	A few final touches required to be perfect	Clean, neat, & commercial in appearance
Method of building	Used own method, "Cut & Try"	Made poor use of the methods shown	Followed correct methods most of the time	Used the demonstrated methods
Tools	Careless with tools	Used tools correctly most of the time	Correctly used tools at all times	Correctly used & cared for tools at all times
Materials	Wasteful & careless with materials	Wasteful with materials at times	Usually careful of materials	Conserves materials at all times
Accuracy of work	Fails to meet specifications	Work is approximately correct	A few measurements are off	Meets all of the specifications
Working time	No effort made to use time wisely	Time used fairly well	Wasted small amount of time	Used time to best advantage

SAFETY PROGRAM

Safety education is a major part of the instructional program in woodworking. It should be a part of every lesson. The safety program should include: general safety policies, specific safety rules for each tool or machine, posters, tests, and other material based on correct technical information, good judgment, and positive behavior outcomes. A list of general safety policies for your laboratory, such as is given in the visual masters, should be posted and explained to the students.

Safety Checklist for Instructors

*Yes
or
No*   *Attitude and Personality*

_____ 1. Do I think, speak, and act with regard to safety at all times?

_____ 2. Have I integrated my safety program with what I am teaching in an interesting, logical manner?

_____ 3. Are my students keenly aware that safety is a vital, required part of my program?

_____ 4. Do I immediately curb horseplay and carelessness in the lab at all times?

_____ 5. Have I explained and demonstrated the need for cooperation among students and teacher for certain jobs of lifting, gluing of boards, and carrying of materials?

_____ 6. Am I acquainted with the school laws of my state regarding safety, negligence, etc.?

Lab Dress

_____ 1. If students are required to wear lab coats or aprons, do I insist that they be kept neat, clean, and buttoned or tied at all times?

_____ 2. If students do not wear coats or aprons, do I insist that they refrain from wearing new or loose clothing?

_____ 3. Have I told the students the danger of wearing long-sleeved shirts, neckties, jewelry, etc., and am I on constant guard to see that no one forgets?

Material Storage

_____ 1. Is the material on lumber racks, metal racks, clamp racks, etc., stored neatly and safely at all times?

_____ 2. Are all materials stored in proper, convenient places and not left lying about in haphazard fashion?

_____ 3. Are all material storage places sufficiently lighted?

_____ 4. Do I guard against overstocking racks, shelves, etc.?

Hand Tools

_____ 1. Are my tool panels, tool room, etc., organized in a neat, safe fashion?

_____ 2. Have I told my students the danger of using dull hand tools?

_____ 3. Have I stressed the safety points on the various hand tools during my talks and demonstrations, and am I on constant guard to see that the student participation is done correctly?

_____ 4. Have I explained and demonstrated the correct procedure for carrying sharp-edged tools?

Machinery

_____ 1. Is each machine properly located in respect to space, efficiency, and safety?

_____ 2. Are all cutting edges, belts, pulleys, etc., carefully guarded?

_____ 3. Is there adequate light for the safe operation of each machine?

_____ 4. Are the accessories for each machine placed in the proper location? (Avoid reaching over running machines for needed accessories.)

_____ 5. Are all machine switches guarded and properly painted?

_____ 6. Are all machines clean and properly painted?

_____ 7. Are goggles available for the operator of certain machines, such as grinders, lathes, etc.? Do I insist that goggles be worn when necessary?

_____ 8. Have proper safety rules and demonstrations been shown, studied, and talked about informally for the operation of each machine before any student participation?

_____ 9. Is student participation on each machine an individual affair, whereby each student must qualify by passing tests?

Finishing Room, Acids

_____ 1. Is there proper ventilation in the finishing room?

_____ 2. Is there a special booth for spraying, if much spraying is done?

_____ 3. Are large quantities of combustible materials kept in fireproof rooms or closets?

_____ 4. Are oily rags and waste kept in proper receptacles?

_____ 5. Is the finishing room kept neat and clean at all times?

_____ 6. Are all containers closed tightly and stored away from heat sources?

_____ 7. Are acids and other harmful agents used in the laboratory kept in proper containers and clearly labeled, and are they stored in a safe place?

General Safety Rules

_____ 1. Is the laboratory well lighted, clean, free of grease and oil on the floor, and neatly painted?

_____ 2. Does each machine have an adequate safety lane painted on the floor?

_____ 3. Are all light switches in good working condition and of the right type for each part of the lab (for instance, mercury switches in the finishing room)?

_____ 4. Have all lines and electrical circuits been checked for proper load?

_____ 5. Are all plugs and extension cords in good condition? (No splices or poorly taped wires.)

_____ 6. Am I familiar with all fuse panels for the laboratory? Are proper fuse loads always maintained?

_____ 7. Have the fire extinguishers been checked recently, and are they of the right type for each area in which they are located?

_____ 8. Do I help promote safety by keeping interesting and relevant bulletin board displays?

_____ 9. Do I have a fair knowledge of first aid and what to do in case of an accident?

_____ 10. Is there a good first aid kit at my service in the event I should need it?

_____ 11. Are insurance and accident report papers neatly filed and kept ready (just in case)?

There is no place in the entire school system where a definite program of safety education can be more effectively organized and administered than in the lab. The safety program should make the lab a safe place in which to work and should develop an attitude of safety.

Causes of Accidents

1. Conditions of room and equipment.
   a. Poor lighting.
   b. Improper location of machines.
   c. Unguarded belts, pulleys, gears, leadscrews, cutters, etc.
   d. Floors, passageways, and stockrooms littered with scraps.
   e. Dull tools and machines.
   f. Unguarded switches.
   g. Pushers, jigs, or guards not used.
2. Inefficient instruction
   a. No thought to safety; too much chancetaking.
   b. No machine permit.
   c. Overtime work without supervision.
   d. No thought to proper attitude.
   e. Failure to check faulty machines.

Safety Standards

1. Establish safety regulations. These are to take effect at the beginning of an assignment, and they are to be a continuing policy during the time the individual remains in the lab.
2. Organize detailed lesson plans for each new group of students assigned to machine work.
3. Put the regulations into effect before an accident occurs and insist upon their enforcement.
4. Make certain that students have a full and complete understanding of the regulations.
5. Rigidly enforce the rules of the lab. Students who do not observe the rules should not be allowed to use the machines.
6. Repeat instructions, warnings, cautions, and demonstrations which aim toward accident prevention. A good motto: "Don't take chances—know."
7. Do not allow conversations between students operating any machine. If instructions are necessary, the machine must be stopped.
8. Require students to obtain the instructor's permission before they operate any motorized machine.
9. Permit only one person at a time to operate a given machine.

Machine Operation Permits

Teachers should require machine operation permits to be signed by the students' parents or legal guardians as a prerequisite to the students' use of machines. Such permits should call attention to the fact that the machines are well guarded and that students using them are carefully instructed and supervised.

First Aid

Another means of protecting the student and teacher is first aid training. Many times a small cut or wound will develop into something much more serious because of the lack of first aid. It should be impressed upon the student that, no matter how trivial the accident seems at the time, proper first-aid precautions should be taken. Any accident should be reported through the principal to the school nurse or physician.

Accident Reports

Accident reports should contain the statements of the injured person and all witnesses to the accident as well as the teacher's analysis of the case. The teacher should present a copy of the report to the principal and file a copy.

General Safety Instructions on Machines

When instructing students on the use of machines:
1. Tell them what you want done.
2. Show them the right way to do the job.
3. Test them. Let them practice while you observe; suggest improvements.
4. Check them. Put them to work; check to see that rules are followed . . . and plan on repeating safety instructions often.

Give a discussion in the vicinity of the machines which are to be operated. Stress basic safety practices. A suggested outline for the discussion follows:

Discussion Outline

I. Purpose. The purpose of this discussion is to let you know how to operate machinery correctly —and that means safely! A machine—whatever its size, whatever the power source—does exactly what you direct it to do. Accidents with machines can be very severe, but they can be avoided.
II. Safety practices. Here are a few basic safety tips when working with or around machines of any kind.
   A. Clothing. The clothes you wear are important. Whirling wheels or drive shafts can easily catch floppy clothing, so wear smooth-fitting clothes that will give you needed protection. Avoid any dangling, loose clothes, such as a tie or scarf. Remove watch, rings, and other jewelry which can catch on sharp corners or moving parts. (Describe any special protective equipment, such as goggles or respirators, that should be used.)

B. Guards. Keep guards in place. Almost every machine has an assortment of shafts, pulleys, belts, chain drives, and gears—all moving! Where these parts are exposed to workers, a guard is often placed or built in to prevent you from touching or getting caught in the parts. These guards must never be removed when the machine is operating. They are protection for you. They may be removed when repair, adjustment, or lubrication is necessary, but never when any part is moving. Call the instructor when major adjustments must be made.

C. Know your machine. Safe operators know a lot more about a machine than just how to start and stop it. They know the complete operation, how to make necessary adjustments, and how to lubricate and maintain it. Above all, they know that the machine has limits, so they operate it at a safe, steady speed and don't try to do jobs for which it was not designed. If you have any questions on operating or using a machine, ask the instructor before proceeding further. Do not experiment.

D. Avoid unfamiliar machines. There are many different machines used in this work, and you cannot expect to be an expert with all of them at once. Learn thoroughly the machine that you're assigned to. Meanwhile, avoid those machines which are not directly connected with your work. Many serious accidents have happened because a worker was unfamiliar with the machine.

E. Keep your mind on your work. Pay attention to the job you are doing. Avoid horseplay.

III. Summary. In this brief discussion, we've reviewed the importance of following safe practices when working around machines: wear the right clothing and equipment; keep machine guards in place; know how to operate, adjust, and maintain the machine; avoid unfamiliar machines; keep your mind on your work. Safety around machines—as in all situations—is mostly up to you. You're the one who can think. Learn your machine's operation thoroughly. You do the thinking; let the machine do the work.

CAREER INFORMATION

Careers related to woodworking should be included in every course. Teachers should also get acquainted with the individual student's interest and aptitudes in order to further the student's educational and career goals. Materials concerning careers should be posted on the bulletin board and students should be made aware of career information available in the counseling office, library, and community.

CLEANUP DUTIES AND ASSIGNMENTS

A list of cleanup duties and a separate cleanup assignment sheet for each class should be posted.

Cleanup Duties

General Cleanup Duties
1. Students at each woodworking bench are responsible for that bench being clean.
2. Students at each woodworking bench are responsible for orderly placement of stools.
3. Each student is responsible for putting away the tools that he/she has used.
4. Each student is responsible for keeping his/her scrap pieces off the floor and putting them into waste boxes.

Specific Cleanup Duties
1. Each student is assigned to a specific cleanup job which will be his/her responsibility.
2. Cleanup will be sounded _____ minutes before the end of the period. At that time all work must stop and cleanup begin.
3. When a cleanup job has been done, each student must go to the work station and wait to be dismissed.

Specific Assignments
1. *Finishing room*—Make sure that all projects are put on the shelves. Cabinet top and sink should be clean. All brushes should be cleaned. Storage shelves should be dusted weekly.
2. *Project storage room*—Keep bar and cabinet clamps in neat order, see that shelves or lockers are orderly, see that projects on the floor are stored neatly, and dust storage shelves weekly.
3. *Lumber rack*—Keep neat daily.
4. *Hand tool cabinet*—See that all of the tools are there and in place; check at both beginning and end of period and report any that are missing. Also dust cabinet weekly.
5. *Power hand tool cabinet*—See that all of the tools are there and in place; check at both the beginning and end of the period and report any that are missing. Also dust cabinet weekly.
6. *Glue bench*—Clean top daily, keep hand screws in order, and keep glue cabinet in order. Also dust tops of power panels daily.
7. *Oil stone and bench grinder*—Inspect and clean daily.

8. *Jig saw and band saw*—Inspect and dust daily.
9. *Drill presses and drill cabinet*—Inspect drill presses and dust them daily. Keep cabinet clean and in order.
10. *Wood lathes and lathe tool panel*—Inspect and dust daily. Also make sure that all lathe tools are in their respective places in the tool panel.
11. *Surfacer*—Inspect and dust daily.
12. *Sander and sanding supply cabinet*—Inspect and dust sander daily. Also make sure that cabinet is clean and orderly.
13. *Radial saw*—Inspect and dust daily.
14. *Jointer*—Inspect and dust daily. Turn off power at end of the period.
15. *Table saws*—Inspect and dust daily.

Cleanup Assignments and Procedures

Every student in the class has a responsibility regarding cleanup. The cleanup procedure is as follows:
1. Cleanup is sounded by the superintendent. There will be _____ minutes for cleanup.
2. Return projects and materials to proper storage.
3. Return tools and machine accessories to proper cabinets.
4. Brush off benches.
5. Perform individual cleanup assignments.
6. Check out with superintendent.
7. Await formal dismissal by teacher.

Lab Personnel Plan

SUPERINTENDENT _____

1. Sound cleanup.
2. Oversee all supervisors and check final cleanup at the end of the class period and report to the instructor.

ASSISTANT SUPERINTENDENT _____

1. Be responsible for superintendent's duties if he/she is late or absent.
2. Check auxiliary room cleanup.
3. Assign alternates in case of absences.

TOOL SUPERVISORS

Hand tools cabinet _____

Portable power tool cabinet _____

Hardware cabinet _____

Machine accessories cabinet _____

Lathe accessories cabinet _____

1. Beginning of class: Unlock tool cabinets and check to see that all tools are in place.
2. End of class: Check to see that all tools are returned to their proper places. Lock the cabinet and report to the superintendent that your responsibilities are completed.

BENCH SUPERVISOR _____

ASSISTANT _____

1. Return all tools left on benches to the proper cabinet.
2. Brush off all benches.
3. Close all vises and place the handles in a vertical position.
4. Report to the superintendent that your responsibilities are completed.

FINISHING ROOM SUPERVISOR

1. Check out paint brushes and see that they are returned in good condition.
2. See that all rags and papers are properly disposed of.
3. See that all benches are clean.
4. See that all cans are covered and returned to proper storage.
5. See that all spray equipment is clean and properly stored.
6. Clean the sink.
7. Report to the superintendent that your responsibilities are completed.

ASSEMBLY AND DRYING ROOM SUPERVISOR

1. Clean all benches.
2. See that projects do not obstruct floor area.
3. Return all clamps and glue to proper storage.
4. Clean the sink.
5. Report your responsibilities as having been completed to the superintendent.

LABORATORY AREA SUPERVISORS

MACHINE AREA 1

Responsible for these machines: _____

_____

_____

1. Remove all sawdust and chips from machines.
2. Return all accessories to the proper storage.
3. Report to the superintendent that your responsibilities are completed.

MACHINE AREA 2

Responsible for these machines: _____

_____

_____

1. Remove all sawdust and chips from machines.
2. Return accessories to the proper storage.
3. Place a safety push stick on all circular saws.
4. Report to the superintendent that your responsibilities are completed.

MATERIAL STORAGE AND LUMBER ROOM SUPERVISOR

1. See that all lumber and plywood are returned to the proper storage area.
2. See that all scrap cuttings are deposited in the proper containers.
3. Return usable abrasives to dispenser and fill dispenser as necessary.
4. Clean lumber storage area.
5. Report your responsibilities as having been completed to the superintendent.

PLANNING FOR A SUBSTITUTE TEACHER

Sometimes it is necessary to be away from the laboratory for one or more days because of illness, for professional development, or for personal reasons. Arrangements should be in place so that a substitute teacher (with or without a background in woodworking) can operate the facility. Make certain that good instruction continues even though students may not be able to use tools and machines. Here are the procedures to follow:

Security Duties

- Make sure that all projects, tools, machines, and materials are properly stored.

- Lock all windows, doors, closets, cabinets, and electrical circuits at the end of the day.
- Make sure another teacher (preferably a technology teacher) is acquainted with your facilities.

Information for the Substitute Teacher

Have a folder ready that is clearly marked *"Substitute Teacher."* Leave it on your desk or with the principal. It should include the following:
- Location of keys to all lab facilities.
- All standard forms used by the school.
- All forms used in your laboratory.
- Lab seating plan.
- Attendance book.
- Emergency drill procedures (fire, tornado, etc.).
- General instructions on what students can and cannot do.
- Course of study, including a copy of the textbook and student workbook. Students may be required to use a student workbook and answer the questions.
- Time schedule with dates so that the substitute teacher will know the kind of activities that students should be involved in during your absence. (Inform students that the work done when you are away will be graded and counts towards their final grade.)
- Instructions on how to secure the classroom and lab at the end of each day.
- Instructions on where to leave all students' paperwork, grade sheets, attendance records, etc.
- List of persons and places to contact in the school—principal, counselor, nurse, medical office, etc.
- List of alternative lessons that can be given by the substitute:
A. Audiovisual lesson plans on such topics as lumbering; furniture and cabinet design; safety; career opportunities; manufacture of plywood, hardboard, etc. Each lesson should include:
   1. Time required.
   2. Name of topic.
   3. Objective.
   4. Titles of audiovisual materials. These may be filmstrips or films. Give exact name and location of these items.
   5. Equipment. Give specific instructions on where screens, film or filmstrip projectors, extra bulbs, etc., are located. Tell if student help is available for operating the equipment.
   6. Introduction to the lesson.
   7. Presentation of topics.
   8. Application. This may be done later by the regular teacher.
   9. Evaluation. A written test may be included with the lesson.
B. If a substitute teacher has woodworking skills, the teacher may demonstrate some unusual aspect of woodworking not included in the regular course outline.
C. Various classroom lessons that involve use of textbook and student guides.
D. Wood identification test.
E. Maintenance assignments.
F. Handwork that may be done on projects.

CHECKLIST FOR TEACHERS

It is difficult for teachers to keep in mind the many things they need to do as they begin a year's work. For this reason the following list of reminders has been prepared. The list is not all-inclusive, but it should help bring to mind factors which are important. It is suggested that you underline or make notes on important points that you wish to emphasize.

1. *Inventory*—Remember to ask at once for an inventory of your lab and supplies. If no inventory is available, be sure to make one immediately and file a copy with the superintendent, supervisor, or principal. Such a procedure may save many embarrassing moments later on in the year and will make a good impression.
2. *Cleanup schedule*—Have you organized a cleanup schedule? This should be done during the first few days of the term.
3. *Lab personnel system*—What about your lab personnel system? Will you have a general supervisor, tool supervisor, and supply supervisor? Will you have one general manager?
4. *Records*—What system will you employ in accounting for the materials used by students? Card system, plan of procedure record, material supervisor, day-to-day list—these are some of the possibilities. Find out early what reports must later be made so that necessary data may be accumulated.
5. *Storage*—Do you have adequate space for the storage of students' materials and projects? Look into this matter before anything is lost.
6. *Student records*—Have you examined the student records in the main office? Remember that it is very important to have as complete and detailed a record of each student as possible. Again, a card system may be advantageous; a cumulative record folder would be better if

there is room for filing these. Notes on individual students should be entered from time to time. They will prove helpful on many future occasions.

7. *Filing system*—Do you have a system for filing working drawings of projects, catalogs and price lists, book lists, and related information? You can get an abundance of free instructional material from manufacturing and sales firms.

8. *Organized plan for continual improvement*—When you have thoroughly studied your laboratory as a place of work and instruction, you should formulate an organized plan for continual improvement of the physical aspects. This should be in writing and a copy should be filed with your principal or other supervisor. The following few points are merely suggestions: future rearrangement of lab layout, additions, painting, resurfacing, new equipment, lighting, and soundproofing.

9. *Possibilities in the community*—Have you contacted individuals and firms who may be cooperative in your program? Are there any establishments to which a visit would be educational for the students? Sometimes it is possible to obtain materials or tools that will add considerably to your teaching. Sometimes gifts of material are made by interested companies.

10. *Advertising*—Your work, as to objectives and practices, must be given publicity. If you have something worthy to offer, advertise this to students and to the public. Remember that the school paper, the local paper, radio, etc., are appropriate avenues.

11. *Objectives*—Have you formulated objectives for each of your courses? Put these in writing to show any person who may be interested. The principal may require these statements.

12. *Examples of your work*—Let the students see some examples of your own work. Show them that you can do more than talk, that you are skillful as well as informed. Have a display ready the first day of school to "sell" yourself and your programs.

13. *Materials fee*—If you must charge the students for materials, set up the system before any projects are made. One method is to have a "Project Permission Card" which the student fills out before he or she begins a project. This should give you and the student an estimate of the cost even before the project has been started. This would be followed up later, of course, by a detailed bill of materials listing actual costs.

14. *Price list*—As soon as possible, post a price list of the materials that must be paid for by students. They should see this before beginning their projects. There will then be little excuse for their making things which they cannot afford.

15. *Displays*—See whether it will be possible to have a display placed in the school where examples of work done in the lab can be exhibited. Perhaps a corner of the library can be used, or a window section or wall case. By having exhibits which are regularly changed, you will build up interest while presenting something that is educational.

16. *Bulletin boards*—Remember to utilize your bulletin boards to the utmost. The effectiveness of bulletin material is enhanced by posting a small amount at a time and by changing the material often. One method of managing this responsibility is to appoint a student whose duty it is to change the bulletin board material every week. The student will keep you aware of the necessity of getting new materials.

17. *Safety rules*—Have you made out the safety rules or safety specifications for using the tools and machines in the lab? Several industrial firms, schools, and city and state departments publish statements or bulletins concerning safety as applied generally in woodwork or to specific processes or machines.

18. *Discipline cases*—Take a firm stand with early discipline cases that arise. Almost invariably the students will test you during the first few class periods. Your position should be made known at once and there should be little question as to who is in charge. Individual cases will have to be handled differently, but they should be handled directly. However, discipline cases should not make you lose your friendly attitude.

19. *Budget*—Have you inquired as to whether you will have a budget to manage? What are the procedures you must go through in order to spend money? How much may you spend? Is it a matter of specific or blanket requisition, or may you buy for cash when necessary? These are a few of the pertinent financial questions that should be answered to your satisfaction early.

20. *Tangible goals*—Are your students aware of what they will get from your courses? Have you set up any tangible goals which look feasible to the students? Too often we take this for granted and students do not know what to expect as logical outcomes of instruction.

21. *Projects*—Will you permit all students to make what they wish, or will you specify or approve? Perhaps it will be better to follow a middle-of-the-road policy and to do some of each.

22. *Bibliographies*—Do you have bibliographies of books published in the various technical fields? These may be obtained or developed with cooperation of teacher-training institutions or publishing houses. The local city or school librarian might be interested in such a project.

23. *Catalogs and price lists*—Catalogs and price lists of lab materials and equipment should be at hand.

24. *Grading*—Do you know how you are going to grade your students? It is a good idea to commit the plan to writing in order that your grading will be as objective as possible. What weight will be assigned to manipulative work? How about tests and outside assignments? These are but two of the many questions that should be considered long before marking is to be done.

25. *Career information*—In what manner are you going to impart career information? Much is expected of the teacher in this respect, and all too often very little is done. Every technology teacher should have had a foundational guidance course.

26. *English*—How good is your English? Many technology teachers in the past have been notorious for being unable to express themselves as effectively as other teachers. Concentrate on making your oral and written expression conform to the rules of good usage.

27. *Free periods*—Are you going to permit students to work in the lab during their free periods? Perhaps no definite rule can be made, but you should consider the matter before the question arises.

MAINSTREAMING SPECIAL NEEDS STUDENTS

Mainstreaming is the placing of special needs students in regular classroom programs. For technology programs, mainstreaming has heightened significance. Such programs offer to the special needs student the benefit of a relatively unrestricted learning environment. It is important to understand that special needs students will need to develop the same skills as other students. To enable them to develop these skills, you may need to adapt your teaching practices to meet their needs.

Some students, because of vision or hearing difficulties, may require special assistance to complete work in the classroom or lab. The special needs of these students may require you to offer particular assistance. Some special needs students may have vision or hearing difficulties. Others may have limited motor skills. Such handicaps may require you to alter slightly your classroom presentations and lab demonstrations. To help the special needs student feel comfortable in your program, you need to follow several simple practices.

If you have students who have difficulty with vision, you should offer them the opportunity to explore your lab area. This will allow them to become familiar with the layout. Ideally, this should be done before the course is started. Seat these students toward the front of the classroom. Be attentive to their difficulties in your lectures. Do not, for example, make vague references during lectures and demonstrations. Be specific. Remember to identify clearly each part and operation.

Students with hearing difficulties may also be mainstreamed into your courses. When lecturing to hearing-impaired students, speak distinctly and in a normal tone of voice. In conducting lab activities, remember to modify lab procedures that depend on hearing skills.

Students with physical disabilities may require special assistance. You should try to set up your lab and classroom to eliminate physical barriers. Equipment should be moved to accommodate wheelchair travel. Machine control and work areas should be arranged to give easy access. Ramps should replace stairs.

Meeting the needs of a handicapped student requires common sense and adaptability. It can also require creativity and the imagination to modify projects and activities to develop the skills of the handicapped student. In responding to the requirements of the special needs student, remember that the student is to be challenged, not merely accommodated.

CAREERS

The text contains seven career essays. Each is titled "Thinking about a Career." Each focuses on one particular occupation. The seven occupations actually detailed were selected on the basis of their appeal to the readers of the text.

These essays are meant to provoke in the student a curiosity—in this case, a curiosity about the world of work. They are not directly intended to inspire the reader to go into one of the fields discussed; rather, they are meant to provoke some thought on possible career choices. Above all, the essays are designed to reinforce (or perhaps introduce) the knowledge that the self-employed, the entrepreneurs, are an important segment of the American work force. The diversity of their job skills and the strength of their ambition have been two of the mainsprings of technological progress throughout our nation's history. It is hoped that these essays will raise for their readers questions that will lead them into a more personal exploration of possible career choices.

The gaining of successful employment is essential. In order to gain entry into the job market, the student must have certain information. He or she must, for example, know how to locate information on the latest trends in the job market. The student must also be able to identify the skills needed to gain employment in a specific field.

Refer the students to the latest edition of the *Occupational Outlook Handbook,* published by the U.S. Department of Labor. This book is available in most libraries.

You can encourage students to begin thinking about a career choice by assigning the following activities.

Activity 1

1. Ask students to use library materials to do research on careers they wish to pursue in the future.
2. Have each student write a short report on the career he or she has chosen. The report should cover the necessary training, skills, and education. It also should discuss working conditions, opportunities for advancement, and expected salary.
3. If possible, each student might contact a person employed in the chosen career. They might interview this person regarding the answers to the questions presented above.
4. The students should hand in their reports. If time allows, you might ask volunteers to share their information in a short oral report to the class.

Activity 2

This exercise will familiarize students with the information presented in a job ad in the classified section.
1. Ask each student to bring to class the job market classified section of a newspaper.
2. Have each student select two job openings from the classified section. Ask him or her to complete the job search questionnaire by referring to the two classified ads chosen. (The job search questionnaire is among the reproducibles. It may be duplicated.)

CONSUMER AWARENESS

The technological nature of modern industry has assured a nearly limitless variety of goods and services. There may be, for example, several different types of a single product, each type varying from the other by only the smallest features. The technological advances of the postwar years have resulted in product offerings that are wide and varied. There are now more goods and services available than at any other time in the history of the world. Because of expanded technology and a wide range of products and services, the average American citizen enjoys a life-style exceeding that of any of those who have lived before. Even Renaissance kings were without many of the comforts we now consider commonplace.

To those who have always lived in a society that prizes free choice and the free enterprise system of capitalism, a wide choice of goods is not unfamiliar. What sometimes is lacking, though, is the consumer's ability to choose between a need and a want. Basically, an item that is needed is essential for survival. For example, food, housing, and clothing are all items that are needed. Generally, the need for such essential items is universal, human needs being the same. All people need food, shelter, and clothing.

Items that are merely wanted, or desired, are often not needed. Some of these items are frivolous, sometimes being bought to satisfy the desire simply to have them. Once purchased, the item may quickly be forgotten, and may even go unused.

It has always been difficult for people to save money. Human nature and the acquisitive instinct have prompted people in every age of history to spend what they have earned on what they do not need. The wider the product choice and the larger the amount of disposable income (money that can be spent), the greater the chance that the consumer will make an unwise purchase.

In your class, relate the principles of wise and careful buying to the purchase of wood and other building materials. Mention that the technology of the forest products industry has presented to the American consumer the widest possible variety of building materials, including an array of exotic hardwoods. Mention also that many of these materials are expensive. In some cases, a material costing less will provide the same durability and— sometimes—the same general quality.

Stress that any product, before it is bought, should be carefully evaluated on the basis of cost and quality. The free enterprise system that characterizes our economic structure thrives on competition. Many manufacturers can develop and market similar products. The practice of critical judgment and careful buying by consumers will encourage a healthy flow of quality goods into the marketplace. It also will discourage the manufacture and marketing of inferior and mediocre goods. The keen awareness of consumers will ensure that the goods and services in the American marketplace are characterized by the quality that has been the hallmark of our manufacturing tradition.

THE DEVELOPMENT OF LEADERSHIP

Our society has always prized resourcefulness and initiative. These qualities were essential to the westward expansion of the American frontier and the early shaping of the values of the infant Republic. Some of the values of our American culture have been shaped by our history which, especially in its early days, required strong decision and firm enterprise. The events that are to us now simply history required fast commitments and unwavering resolution from those who took part in them.

Though the accidentals of historical influence may change, its basic forces remain much the same. This, by no surprise, results in problems and challenges for our society that are as puzzling and difficult as those posed for our ancestors. Because ours is a democratic society, every man and woman is prompted to develop to the fullest those skills and abilities that will lend themselves to the betterment of our society. In this development is found the germ of leadership.

Good leaders are characterized by effective communication, firmness of will, singleness of purpose, and moral integrity. While, it seems, these qualities are more readily apparent in some, all of us can develop, in some degree, the skills needed for effective leadership. Mention to the students that membership in student clubs—such as VICA or ITSA—can help develop leadership ability. A club, by its nature—bringing together as it does individuals with a single common interest—has perhaps less diversity than society generally. Still, it offers students an opportunity to practice effective communication and learn the skills needed to work within a group, such as a committee. Stress to your students that the valuable qualities of leadership are often exercised in the most quiet situations. Each student throughout his or her adult life, will be given opportunities to exert the force of leadership to bring about a decision, resolve a crisis, or prompt an action.

Lead your students in a class discussion of effective leaders in our nation's history. Prompt the students to identify those qualities of an effective leader. Discuss the relationship of leadership to active participation in a democratic society.

Answers to Review Questions in Text

Chapter 1

1. Based on discoveries in science, deals with the use of tools, depends on various forms of energy as a source of power.
2. Input device, central processing unit, display device, disk drive, printer.
3. Complicated electronic circuitry on a silicon base with tiny switches joined by "wires."
4. RAM and ROM.
5. Fast, accurate, eliminates repetition.
6. A program that tells the computer what to do and how to do it.
7. Truss design, cabinet design.
8. Control unit, tape, machine, feedback device.
9. Hazardous, monotonous, or precise work.
10. Light Amplification by Stimulated Emission of Radiation.
11. A laser transmitter sends a thin column of light to a receiver. Alignment of the indicator light indicates the placement of survey stakes.
12. Discover your talents, interests, and career potential; learn to use tools and machines; learn about good design; learn to judge the quality of wood products; enjoy the satisfaction of planning and building a product.
13. Answers will vary.

Chapter 2

1. Lumber with 30 to 300 percent moisture.
2. Lumber with a moisture content of 19 percent or less.
3. $13/16$ inch thick.
4. No.
5. Plain-sawed or quarter-sawed.
6. Surfaced two sides.
7. White, green, and black.
8. Easy to work, glue, and finish.
9. Red or white.
10. Walnut.
11. Unfinished mahogany.
12. Tough, strong, easy to work, polishes well.
13. No. Honduras and Africa.
14. Good wear-resisting qualities.
15. Colonial and contemporary.
16. 300.
17. Red oak, white oak.
18. Holds paint and enamel well, easily worked, finishes smoothly.
19. White, yellowish brown.
20. Cabinetwork, furniture, veneers, gunstocks. Beautiful, strong, durable, stiff.
21. Brown heartwood and a nearly white sapwood.
22. Lumber and plywood manufacture.
23. Lightweight, moderately hard, strong. Redwood is harder and more resistant to decay.

Chapter 3

1. An outline, shape, or plan of something.
2. Function, appearance, sound construction.
3. Straight, curved, jagged, zigzag.
4. A solid form created by variation and combinations of the four basic shapes.
5. Formal and informal.
6. No. The sides are all of the same size.
7. Stress on one feature.
8. Answers will vary.
9. It may help to identify construction problems.
10. A list of the pieces you will need, with their dimensions.

Chapter 4

1. Pictorial and working.
2. Pictorial.
3. No.
4. By means of hidden lines.
5. Perhaps, if it is not too large.
6. Dual dimensioning (customary and metric) and metric dimensioning with a customary readout chart.

Chapter 5

1. Plan your work, then work your plan.
2. The needed materials; needed tools and equipment; steps that will be followed and their sequence.
3. Pine.
4. One.
5. Seven pieces of wood, plus hangers and wood screws.
6. Working.
7. A list of needed materials, with their finished dimensions.
8. One-quarter inch is added to the width in making a stock-cutting list.
9. No. (Length is measured from end to end. On a wide board cut to a short length, the width might be longer.)
10. 10 board feet.
11. One dollar.

Chapter 6

1. The length of the arm from the elbow to the tip of the middle finger.

2. Customary and metric.
3. Metre, kilogram, litre.
4. Smaller.
5. System International.
6. Bench rule, folding rule.
7. It can be extended to a length of over 6 feet.
8. To locate the center of a circle.
9. Square, marker, gauge.
10. Rule, square, marking gauge, level, protractor. Answers will vary.
11. Sloyd knife.
12. Four.
13. To protect the pieces to be clamped.
14. If a short length of stock is needed, hold the rule on edge.
15. Hold a rule at an angle across the face of the stock until the inch marks evenly divide the space.

Chapter 7
1. Everyone has an equal responsibility.
2. It will influence your work habits.
3. Remove all extra clothing. Roll up your sleeves and put on a shop apron.
4. It can catch in a machine.
5. Answers will vary.
6. Careless or incorrect procedures.
7. Answers will vary.
8. To assure safe and healthful working conditions.

Chapter 8
1. Craftspeople, technicians, professionals.
2. Carpenters.
3. Answers will vary.
4. One or two years of training at a technical institute or junior college.
5. Answers will vary.

Chapter 9
1. Crosscut saw.
2. Ripsaw.
3. The set makes the saw kerf wider than the blade itself, preventing the blade from buckling.
4. It makes a coarser cut.
5. A chisel.
6. Answers will vary.
7. The board will not split as readily when the cut is completed.
8. 45 degrees.
9. Draw up. The saw will not jump or nick the wood as readily.
10. The line.
11. The cut actually made by the saw blade.
12. To cut the small wood fibers.

13. This occurs most frequently in cutting a long piece of stock to width.
14. Use a wedge.
15. Hold the end of the board as you make the last few cuts.
16. Place the material on edge with guide boards securely clamped at the top and bottom. Make sure the distance between the guide boards is just equal to the width of the saw teeth. Also, be sure the finish (good) side of the material is facing you.

Chapter 10
1. Jack; smooth; fore and jointer.
2. Body, base, frog, adjusting nut, lateral plane lever, double plane iron.
3. 1. Sight along the edge. A sharp blade will not reflect any light.
   2. Cut a piece of paper with it.
   3. Let the cutting edge rest on your nail and then push it lightly. If the blade clings to the nail, it is sharp. If it slides easily, it needs sharpening, or whetting.
4. $1/16$ inch.
5. It stiffens and strengthens the blade and serves as a chip breaker.
6. Insert the double plane iron in the plane with the bevel side down. Watch for the following:
   1. Do not hit the cutting edge on the body of the plane as you insert it over the frog.
   2. Make sure that the slot in the plane iron cap fits over the little Y adjustment.
   3. Check to see that the roller on the lateral adjustment slips into the slot of the plane iron.
   4. Pull the little thumb-adjusting cam on the lever cap up at right angles. Then slip the lever cap over the lever cap screw on the frog. Push the thumb-adjusting cam down to fasten the plane iron securely in the plane. If it must be forced, unscrew the lever cap screw just a little bit. Tighten it a little if it is too loose.
7. This is done with the brass knurled knob.

Chapter 11
1. That surface that is free of flaws and with the most interesting grain.
2. Yes.
3. Place two parallel pieces of wood across the grain, one on each end of the board. Then sight along the top of the first parallel. If you can see one end of the second parallel, you know that the board has a wind. Another method is to

place the board on a level surface to see if the board rocks on two corners.

4. It will dull the blade.
5. To remove wind at the beginning of the board, take a partial cut there. Begin the stroke as before. Then as you plane along the board as far as you think necessary, slowly lift the handle to finish the cut.

   To take the wind out of the end of the board, start the partial cut in the center of the board. Begin with the handle held away from the surface. Gradually lower the handle as you begin the forward motion.
6. Face surface or face side.

Chapter 12

1. In planing a long edge.
2. The edge that is truest.
3. With a vise and a hand screw.
4. In planing an edge you may hold the handle of the plane the same way as for surface planing. To use a second method, place your thumb around the back of the knob with your other fingers curled under the bottom. In this way you can use your fingers along the face side to guide the plane.
5. High spots should be removed, the edge should be cut square with the face surface and straight along its entire length.
6. A gauge used to transfer measurements to the stock. It has a scale along the beam, a small spur, and a thumbscrew.
7. No, the measurement should always be rechecked.
8. No.
9. The board should be ripped to within $1/8$ to $1/16$ inch of the layout line.
10. The last cut you make should just split the dent made by the marking gauge.

Chapter 13

1. Because the tips of the wood fibers are being cut off.
2. It is smaller. Also, the plane iron rests at a lower angle than in other planes.
3. A block plane can be chosen for model work.
4. 1. Plane about halfway across the stock. Then lift the handle of the plane slowly. Begin at the other end and do the same thing. Check for squareness with the working face and working edge.
   2. Plane a short bevel on the waste edge of the stock. Then begin from the other side to plane all the way across.

3. Get a piece of scrap stock exactly the same thickness as the piece you are working. Lock it in the vise just ahead of the piece you are planing. In this way you have actually extended the end grain. Then you can plane all of the way across the end grain without fear of splitting out the piece.

Chapter 14

1. From the piece of metal that stiffens the saw.
2. The dovetail saw has a narrower blade and finer teeth.
3. A piece of wood with a hook stop on opposite surfaces of each end. The wide stop goes over the edge of the bench. The piece to be sawed is held against the shorter stop.
4. Yes.
5. $1/16$ inch.
6. Ripsaw.
7. Care must be taken that the wood does not splinter.

Chapter 15

1. 1. *Animal,* or *hide glue* is made from hoofs, hides, bones, and other animal parts.
   2. *Casein glue,* made from milk curd, is available in powdered form.
   3. *Urea-resin adhesive* is made from urea resin and formaldehyde.
   4. *Resorcinol* is made by mixing liquid resin with a powder catalyst.
   5. *Liquid resin polyvinyl glue,* white in color, is excellent for furniture making and repair.
   6. *Contact cement* is a ready-mixed, rubber-type, bonding agent.
   7. *Epoxy cement* is a two-part adhesive that sticks to most materials.
   8. *Hot-melt glues* are supplied in stick or chunk form for use with an electric glue gun.
2. Casein, urea-resin adhesive, resorcinol, contact cement, epoxy cement, hot-melt glues.
3. Liquid resin.
4. The *cabinet* or *bar, clamp* is used for gluing up large surfaces edge to edge and for clamping parts together when assembling projects. One end is adjusted to length by friction or by a pawl. The other end is moved in and out by a screw.
5. Wood.
6. Answers will vary.
7. To prevent warping.
8. Make sure that the grain of all pieces runs in the same direction. Alternate the pieces so that the annular rings face in opposite directions. Try to

match the pieces to form the most interesting grain arrangement.
9. Construction errors will be detected.
10. A layer sufficient to cover the edges completely.
11. Rubber.
12. By careful clamping.
13. So that the pressure will be equally applied.

Chapter 16
1. No.
2. Planer and jointer.
3.   METHOD A
  1. Plane the face surface or side (working face).
  2. Plane the working edge.
  3. Plane the stock to width (second edge).
  4. Plane the stock to thickness (second surface or side).
  5. Plane one end (working end).
  6. Cut stock to length.
  7. Plane other end (second end).
           METHOD B
  1. Plane the face surface (working surface).
  2. Plane the working edge.
  3. Plane one end square with the face surface and joint edge.
  4. Plane stock to width.
  5. Plane stock to thickness.
  6. Cut off stock to length.
  7. Plane other end.
           METHOD C (recommended)
  1. Plane the face surface. Fig. 16–2.
  2. Plane the working edge.
  3. Plane one end square with the face surface and joint edge.
  4. Cut off stock to length and plane other end.
  5. Plane stock to width.
  6. Plane stock to thickness.

Chapter 17
1. Answers will vary.
2. Place one leg over the inch mark. Open the other leg to the correct width. Lock the thumbscrew.
3. Place a pencil eraser over the point to avoid damaging the wood.
4. A measuring device used for laying out large circles.
5. Octagon, eight sides; hexagon, six sides.
6. Find the distance across the octagon. Lay out a square of this size. Set a dividers or *compass* to half the diagonal length across the square. Set the point of the compass at each corner of the square. Strike an arc from one side of the square to the other from each corner. Join the points where the arcs meet the sides of the square.

7. An *ellipse* is a regular curve that has two different diameters. Lay out the two diameters at right angles to each other. Set a dividers equal to half the longest diameter. Place the point of the dividers on point C. Strike an arc to intersect the longest diameter at points X and Y. Place a thumbtack at these two points and another at one end of the shortest diameter. Tie a string around the three thumbtacks. Remove the outside thumbtack and place a pencil inside the string. Hold the pencil at right angles to the paper. Carefully draw the ellipse.
8. When the project is not drawn full size.
9. It makes the transfer of the design much easier.
10. No.
11. A pattern.

Chapter 18
1. A coping saw or a compass saw.
2. Ripsaw.
3. Toward.
4. Twenty to thirty.
5. In the waste stock.
6. A small handsaw with a thin, tapered blade.

Chapter 19
1. It is used to smooth a surface.
2. It was used originally to shape the spokes of wheels.
3. Yes.
4. Finishing the edges of curves and molding irregular shapes.
5. Hold the tool in both hands, with the blade firmly against the wood and the bevel side down. Turn the blade at a slight angle to the work.
6. A rasp is cut with individually shaped teeth.
7. No.
8. A handle must be placed on the tang.
9. It is used like a rasp. Light pressure is applied.

Chapter 20
1. A chamfer is an angular cut only partway across the corner or edge; the bevel is an angle cut completely across the edge.
2. No.
3. Hold the plane or chisel at an angle to the surface, and take a shearing cut across the edge. This will help prevent splitting out the chamfer.
4. By clamping the stock.
5. One that does not extend the whole length of the board.
6. To check the angle.
7. On opposite sides.

Chapter 21

1. Short blades, three or four inches long, with beveled sides.
2. Yes.
3. Hold the chisel with the bevel side against the stock. Grasp the chisel handle in your right hand and the blade in your left. Apply pressure with your right hand. Guide the tool with your left.
4. You can apply the cutting action in two ways. You can force the blade into the stock parallel to the wood. You can also make a shearing cut, with the blade moving from right to left as it cuts. You will find that straight cutting takes more pressure. Also, it is more convenient to hold the tool in your left hand and pound with the mallet held in your right hand.
5. When making light, paring cuts with the chisel, turn the tool around with the flat surface next to the wood. Hold the blade between your thumb and forefinger to guide it in taking these cuts.
6. Work from one side about halfway across the stock. Work from both sides to the finished line, leaving the center higher. With light paring cuts, bring the center down to the line. Clean out the corners with the chisel.
7. Hold the chisel in one hand with the flat side toward the shoulder. Draw the chisel across as you would a knife.
8. No.
9. Because you are cutting with the grain.
10. Begin at one corner of the stock. Tip the handle to one side, rotate the handle to get a shearing cut. Work toward the center.
11. Yes.
12. A gouge is a chisel with a curved blade.
13. With the bevel on the inside or the outside.
14. An outside bevel gouge.
15. With the grain.

Chapter 22

1. In low relief carving, the background is cut away to form the surface design. The carving is fairly shallow.
2. Wood sculpture.
3. White pine, genuine mahogany, Philippine mahogany, walnut.
4. Skew or chisel; parting tool; veiner; gouges and fluters; knives.
5. Some general procedures are the same, though there are differences. The tools, for example may be guided differently, depending on the carving operation.
6. The PEG treatment protects wood against warping and checking. It is outlined in the chapter.

Chapter 23

1. Ash, hickory, birch, and oak.
2. Heating tube, form, C-clamps, parallel handscrews, thin sheet metal.
3. The wood will split.

Chapter 24

1. The process of building up the thickness or width of material by gluing together several layers.
2. Warpage resistance; strength.
3. Refer to the detailed list of steps included in the chapter.
4. Refer to the detailed plan of procedure included in the chapter.

Chapter 25

1. Twist drill.
2. It is a hand tool. The drill is held in place by a three-jawed chuck capable of holding round shanks. The drill is operated by means of a crank fixed to a gear arrangement.
3. If right-handed, hold the handle in the left hand and turn the crank with your right hand.
4. A bit used for holes that are $1/4$ to $1 1/4$ inch.
5. On the tang.
6. A tool that can be adjusted with different cutters for diameters from $7/8$ to 3 inches. Adjust the cutter until the distance from the spur to the feed screw equals the radius of the hole. Fasten the bit in the brace and make sure the work is held tightly. Use just enough pressure to make a cut. After the feed screw shows through, reverse the stock and cut from the other side.
7. Boring a hole partway into thin board or enlarging an existing hole.
8. Box rachet, chuck, bow, handle, quill, head.
9. For drilling in corners or other tight places.
10. Sight along the board or use a try square.
11. No, you should turn the wood over to complete the hole.
12. A depth gauge prevents a drill from penetrating the stock to its full length.
13. A depth gauge can be made by boring through a piece of wood or dowel rod, exposing the auger bit to the correct depth.
14. To bore a hole at an angle, first adjust a sliding T-bevel to the required angle. Use this as a guide. Start the auger bit as you would for straight boring until the screw feeds into the wood. Then tilt the bit so that it is parallel to the blade of the T-bevel.
15. Adjust the cutter until the distance from the spur to the feed screw equals the radius of the hole.

Chapter 26

1. Sharp cutting tools cut easily and cleanly.
2. It can be reground.
3. 20 degrees for softwoods; 25 to 30 degrees for hardwoods.
4. At an angle of 30 to 35 degrees.
5. Place it in a vise with the cutting edge showing. Hold a file flat against the side of the scraper and take a few strokes. Use a fine file to drawfile the edge until it is square with the sides of the scraper. Hold the burnishing tool at an angle of about 85 degrees.
6. To test for sharpness, hold the plane iron with the cutting edge down and allow the edge to rest lightly on the thumbnail. As you move the tool, it will tend to "bite" into the nail if it is sharp. It will slide across easily if it is dull. Another method is to look carefully at the edge. A sharp edge cannot be seen. If it is dull, a thin white line can be seen.
7. Grind the screwdriver with a slight taper on each side and the end flat.

Chapter 27

1. By adding dowels.
2. Birch.
3. They reinforce it.
4. The diameter of the dowel should never be more than half the thickness of the wood.
5. Yes, about $1/8$ inch.
6. A doweling jig ensures that you bore the dowel holes in the correct place.
7. See pp. 214-215.
8. The joint would be misaligned.
9. A machine is used to cut slots; glue is applied; the biscuit is inserted; the pieces are clamped.

Chapter 28

1. A rabbet joint is a slot cut at the end or edge of one piece into which the end or edge of a second piece fits. It is used in drawer construction, boxes, and cabinet frames.
2. Superimposing is the placement of two boards, one atop the other. The bottom board is placed on the bench with its face surface down. The top board is placed directly over the first, with the face surface of the second piece flush with the end grain of the first.
3. A sharp pencil, a knife, a try square.
4. By marking them with corresponding numbers.
5. Backsaw.
6. When excess stock needs to be pared out. Regardless, the chisel will need to be used to trim the joint.
7. Drive them in at a slight angle.

Chapter 29

1. A groove cut across a grain of wood.
2. A rabbet joint is always used on corners.
3. In the waste stock.
4. A router plane has blades of different widths. A router plane can be used to remove the waste stock.
5. Check the dado joint with a combination square to make sure it has the same depth throughout.
6. Plane the edge of the second piece.
7. Additional strength and stiffness.
8. The blind dado joint is shown in Fig. 29–11.
9. It does not show from the front.

Chapter 30

1. End lap: screen doors, chair seats, construction of flush corners. Middle-lap: screen doors, cabinets, house framing. Cross-lap: furniture, when two pieces must cross and be flush on the surface. Half-lap: to make a longer piece of stock from two shorter pieces.
2. Cross-lap.
3. A right angle.
4. Measure from the face surface.

Chapter 31

1. It is weak.
2. Picture frames, clock cases.
3. The miter box has slots that allow a saw to be adjusted at an angle from 30 to 90 degrees.
4. 45 degrees.
5. Do not let the stock slip.
6. With a spline, dowel, key, or feather.
7. Miter and corner clamp, frame clamp, special spring clamp.
8. Refer to the chapter, where this is discussed in detail.

Chapter 32

1. Yes, it is very strong.
2. The mortise is a rectangular hole into which the tenon, a projecting piece of wood, fits.
3. Blind, open, thru.
4. Answers will vary.
5. The tenon is made half as wide as the total thickness of the piece and about $1/2$ to $3/4$ inch narrower than the total width.
6. Mark the length of the tenon from the end and square a line completely around each piece. Do this on all pieces, then check to see that all of the rails are the same length from shoulder to shoulder. Set the marking gauge to half the thickness of the stock to be removed. Mark a line across the end and down each edge. Add to

this measurement the thickness of the tenon. Check the gauge. Again mark a line across the end and down the sides. Subtract the width of the tenon from the total width of the stock. Divide this amount in half and set this measurement on a marking gauge. From the joint edge of the rail, mark a line across the end and down the side. Add to this measurement the width of the tenon and set the gauge again. Repeat the mark across the end and down the side.

7. Yes.
8. They are the same.
9. No, shoulder cuts are used to remove the waste stock.
10. With an auger bit and brace or with a mortise chisel.
11. With adhesives.

Chapter 33
1. It will have the same shape, being like a box turned on its end or edge.
2. Butt, rabbet, miter.
3. Dado joints, wood cleats, shelf brackets.
4. Dowel pins, metal shelf pins, fixed shelf brackets, adjustable shelf brackets.

Chapter 34
1. By using a wood or metal corner block.
2. Square cleat, square cleat with rabbet and groove, metal tabletop.
3. Slide-block guide, side guide, center guide.
4. Cutting the rail to receive the drawer, making the drawer, making the drawer guide.
5. It should match—in color and grain—the material used for the project.
6. Because they warp less.
7. Mortise and tenon.

Chapter 35
1. Claw, head, wedges, neck, poll, face, cheek, adze eye, handle.
2. Hold the nail set in your left hand with the middle finger against the surface of the work and the side of the nail. Then drive the nail in until it is about $1/16$ inch below the surface.
3. Common, box, casing, finishing.
4. Spikes.
5. It has a slight projection at the top, rather than a head.
6. Grasp the hammer near the head. Tap the head of the nail with the hammer. Remove your fingers from the nail as you continue to strike it with firm, even blows.
7. The head of the hammer.
8. With a nail set.

9. Drill holes slightly smaller than the diameter of the nail. Apply a little wax to the nail and drive it in.
10. Bend the nail over with the grain.
11. Driving nails into the wood at an angle from both sides.

Chapter 36
1. It is stronger. Also, the product can be disassembled.
2. The tip of the screwdriver should be the same width as the diameter of the screw head.
3. The tip should be ground flat, not rounded or beveled. It should not be ground to a sharp edge.
4. The nature and thickness of the material you will be fastening.
5. The diameter increases.
6. Choose a screw that will go at least two-thirds of its length into the second piece.
7. Roundhead screws, sheet-metal screws.
8. It is a hole drilled in the first piece of wood. It allows the screw to be inserted in the first piece without forcing.
9. In softwood, it is drilled only to half the depth to which the screw will go.
10. When flathead screws are used.
11. Turn the screw upside down and fit it in the hold.
12. To conceal screws.
13. To install a screw, hold the blade between your thumb and forefinger. Grasp the handle of the screwdriver in the palm of your hand. Let your thumb and forefinger point toward the shank. Start the screw and then move your left hand up just back of the point of the screwdriver. This will guide the tool and keep it from slipping off the head as the screw is set in place. Continue to turn the screw until it is firmly set.
14. So that the screw is not stripped or the head marred.

Chapter 37
1. Open-grain wood.
2. Before each use—and often during use.
3. 50 to 60 degrees.
4. By keeping the cutting edge flat.
5. Change the direction of the scraping action to match the grain direction.
6. Loosen the adjusting thumbscrew and the clamp thumbscrews. Insert the blade from the bottom, with the bevel side toward the adjusting screw. Make sure the edge of the blade is even with the bottom. This can be done by placing the tool on a wood surface and pressing

the blade lightly against the wood. Tighten the clamp thumbscrews. Bow the blade slightly by tightening the adjusting thumbscrew.

Chapter 38
1. When the wood surface is being finished.
2. No. The abrasives used are flint or quartz, garnet, aluminum oxide, and silicon carbide.
3. Sheets, discs, and belts.
4. A low number for coarse sandpaper; a high number for fine sandpaper.
5. Draw it over the edge of a bench. To tear it, fold it inwards with the abrasive surface inwards.
6. It provides a good backing for most sanding.
7. No.
8. Lock the work in a vise and keep the sanding block square with the sides.
9. By holding the paper in your fingers or the palm of your hand.
10. By wrapping the paper around a broomstick or a tool handle.

Chapter 39
1. You will know how each part fits with the next.
2. The parts must be collected and checked. Protective pieces may need to be made.
3. Yes, to make sure that they fit.
4. Nails, screws, glue.
5. Because the parts will not be clamped.
6. Answers will vary.
7. To ensure that all parts fit properly.
8. Not always.
9. Make sure that the project is square up and has the same height throughout.
10. Just enough, but not too much.
11. Twelve to twenty-four hours.

Chapter 40
1. Answers will vary.
2. A recess cut to accommodate a butt hinge.
3. Its length.
4. Determine how far in the hinge will be from the face of the door. Set a marking gauge to this measurement. Hold the marking gauge against the face side of the door. Mark a line between the two lines to show the position of the hinge. Repeat on the door frame. Then set a marking gauge to the thickness of one leaf. From the edge, mark a line indicating the depth to which the stock must be removed, both on the door and on the frame. This cut in the wood is called a gain.
5. A chisel.

6. Drill and insert one screw. Put the door in position and place the pins in the hinges. Try the door to see how it operates.

Chapter 41
1. Flat-sliced, half-round, quartered, rotary-cut.
2. Flat-slicing.
3. Plain edging, edging with pressure-sensitive adhesive coated with paper, edging coated with adhesive that must be heated.
4. Contact cement, veneer adhesive.
5. Cut sheets of veneer slightly larger, about $1/4$ inch on each side, for each major surface of the project. Coat the surface of the veneer with contact cement, brushing thoroughly. Allow to dry about 30 minutes or until the gloss is gone. Hold the veneer over the surface and align it. Then lower it in place. Roll the surface with a small roller. Place a block of softwood over the veneer, and strike with a hammer until the veneer is in complete contact with the surface. Trim excess material with a knife. Then sand lightly for a square edge. Make sure all sawdust is removed from the edge before applying contact cement for the edging.
6. Permanent bonding does not occur until heat is applied.

Chapter 42
1. A material made up of layers of kraft paper impregnated with resin and a rayon surface paper covered with another kind of resin.
2. It is stain resistant and easily cleaned.
3. Contact cement.
4. It will have a glossy film.
5. No.
6. Use a laminate trimmer and hold the tool at an angle of 20 to 25 degrees for bevel finishing.

Chapter 43
1. Bleaching, staining, filling, the second sealing, the standard finish, rubbing, buffing, and waxing.
2. Natural bristles (hog hair) or synthetic bristles.
3. An oil made from flaxseed. Boiled linseed oil has improved drying qualities as a paint ingredient.
4. Beeswax, paraffin, carnauba wax, and turpentine.
5. A white powder made from lava.
6. A reddish brown or grayish black iron-oxide vehicle that comes from shale.
7. Detailed safety precautions are listed at the end of the chapter.

Chapter 44

1. Glue will not take stain.
2. When the wood has been darkened by casein glue.
3. Shallow dents, chips, gouges.
4. By applying a drop of water to it, placing a wet cloth over it, and pressing with a hot iron.
5. All of the old finish must be removed. The wood must then be wiped with a solvent before being bleached and/or stained.
6. When the color of the wood must be lightened or when stains must be removed.
7. To ensure a fine finish.

Chapter 45

1. Pigment and penetrating.
2. By increasing or decreasing the amount of dye.
3. Cheaper than other stains, a more even color, less likely to fade.
4. One pint of stain will cover about 25 square feet of porous wood.
5. If possible, apply the stain with the wood held in a horizontal position. This will help avoid streaking caused by gravity flow. Always stain the lower surfaces first, beginning at the corner and working out. Begin at the center of the surface. With light strokes, work out toward the edges, brushing on the stain evenly. With each new brushful, begin on the unfinished surface and stroke toward the stained surface. As you near the edges and ends of the wood, brush carefully to keep from spattering the stain. Apply the stain to one small area at a time. Wipe off the excess with a clean, dry cloth.
6. Soak a lint-free rag in linseed oil and rub the end grain with this before applying the stain.
7. Use light strokes, brushing on the stain evenly.
8. Sponge the surface of the wood lightly with water.
9. The stain is brushed on and then wiped off with a cloth.

Chapter 46

1. Liquid filler and paste filler.
2. Paste filler.
3. Turpentine or, if applied under a lacquer finish, lacquer thinner.
4. White lead or pure zinc paste.
5. Mix one part of shellac with six or seven parts of alcohol.

Chapter 47

1. The lac bug.
2. The substance deposited by the lac bug is ground and mixed with denatured alcohol.

3. A mixture of four pounds of shellac with a gallon of alcohol.
4. Orange.
5. Because natural shellac gives to some objects a yellow-orange tint.
6. Dip about one-third of the brush length into the shellac and wipe off the sides of the brush on the container. Begin at the center of a flat surface or near the top of a vertical surface and work out toward the edges. Work quickly and evenly, taking light, long strokes. Do not brush over the same surface several times, as shellac dries very rapidly and becomes sticky.
7. Clean and dry the wood. Wipe the surface with a lint-free cloth dipped in alcohol. Thin the shellac with an equal amount of alcohol. Apply the shellac.

Chapter 48

1. Alkyd resin.
2. No.
3. Dust-free environment; temperature between 70 and 80 degrees Fahrenheit; low humidity.
4. Do not overload the brush, apply the varnish with long, easy strokes. Brush first with the grain and then across the grain. When the brush is dry, brush out the varnish with the grain, using only the tip of the brush. Brush from the center toward the outside edges.
5. Wipe the project with a tack rag to remove dust. Apply the first coat of varnish. Allow to dry. Apply the second and third coats of varnish. Sand each dried coat before applying the next one. Final rubbing. Wax.
6. By rubbing and polishing with special abrasives.
7. A finish of varnish stain. It is useful when time cannot be given to applying many coats of regular varnish.

Chapter 49

1. Spread the oil liberally over the surface with a thick pad or folded cloth. Allow this to soak in until no more is absorbed by the wood. This may take from a few minutes to an hour. Then rub again with the same pad, working additional oil into the pores of the wood. Then wipe off surplus oil with a clean cloth. Allow to dry overnight. Then repeat the process.
2. It dries to a flat nonlustrous film.
3. Apply Sealacell®. Allow to dry overnight. Buff lightly with fine steel wool. Apply Varno-wax. Wipe out with grain. Buff lightly with 3/0 steel wool. Apply Royal finish in same manner as Varno-wax. Buff with fine steel wool.

4. Three.
5. Apply Danish oil finish as follows:
   1. After sanding, apply a quick-dry, alcohol (or water-base), wood stain.
   2. Let dry for about 45 minutes.
   3. Apply liberal amounts of the oil.
   4. Allow the oil to soak into the wood for about 30 minutes, or until penetration stops. Flow on another coat, allowing it to penetrate for about 15 minutes.
   5. Wipe the surface completely dry with a soft, absorbent cloth.
   6. For more luster, let the surface dry for 4 hours.
   7. Dry the wood thoroughly with a clean cloth.
   8. Polish briskly with another cloth.
   9. For additional seen, apply a stain wax after the oil has dried about 24 hours.

Chapter 50
1. Lacquer is a finish composed of nitrocellulose, resins, and solvents.
2. No.
3. By spraying.
4. Load the brush heavily. Apply with long, rapid strokes. Lap the sides of each stroke. Do not attempt to brush the lacquer in.
5. Spray in a well-ventilated room. Start at the side nearest you and spray back and forth, moving toward the rear. Overlap each stroke, turn the project a quarter turn and spray again. Spray several light coats rather than one heavy one.

Chapter 51
1. Enamels are high-gloss paints.
2. Oil-based and latex.
3. They are easily washed.
4. Bottom and edges; legs, inner side first; top edges and frame sides; tabletop.

Chapter 52
1. A paintlike undercoat is applied. A color glaze is applied.
2. No.
3. In the direction of the wood grain.
4. By applying a coat of varnish.

Chapter 53
1. To surface boards to thickness and to smooth rough-cut lumber.
2. Answers will vary. The safety rules are listed in the chapter.

3. $1/8$ inch for rough work; $1/16$ inch for finished work.
4. Turn off the switch. Wait for the cutterhead to stop. Then lower the table.
5. Use a *backing board* that is true, smooth, and at least $3/4$ inch thick. Place the backing board on the bed. Then put the thin stock on it. Adjust for the correct depth of cut, taking into consideration the thickness of the backing board. Then run the two boards together through the surfacer.

Chapter 54
1. Student will provide a sketch.
2. Ripsaw (riptooth), crosscut, combination.
3. The safety precautions are detailed in the chapter.
4. $1/8$ to $1/4$ inch more than the thickness of the stock.
5. Begin with the saw set at less than the total thickness. You may need to run it through several times rather than trying to cut through in one operation.
6. When cutting to narrow widths.
7. Miter gauge.
8. Set the stop rod that is attached to the miter gauge to the correct length; clamp a small block of wood to the ripping fence just in front of the saw blade; fasten a wood extension to the miter gauge and clamp a stop block to it to control the length of cut.
9. Set the gauge to the correct angle and tilt the blade.
10. The stock tends to creep towards the revolving saw as the cut is made.
11. Lay out the groove on the edge of the stock. Set the circular saw to a height equal to the depth of the groove. Adjust the ripping fence to allow the cut to be made just inside the layout line. Hold one surface of the stock firmly against the fence and make a cut. Reverse the stock and make a second cut.
12. The simplest method of cutting the cheek is to clamp the stock to the tenoning jig and position the jig and fence so as to cut out the cheek on the side away from the jig. Then turn the stock around and cut the other cheek without changing the location of the fence.
13. A device that will cut grooves or dadoes from $1/8$ to 2 inches in width.
14. Use an adjustable taper jig. Mark a line to indicate the taper to be cut. Adjust the jig until the line of the taper cut is parallel to the fence.

Chapter 55

1. Depth of cut, angle of cut, bevel cuts.
2. Answers will vary. Safety precautions are discussed in the chapter.
3. To make a straight crosscut, make sure that the arm or track is at right angles to the guide fence. Adjust the depth of cut so that the teeth of the blade are about $1/16$ inch below the surface of the wood table. Set the antikickback device about $1/8$ inch above the work surface.
4. Set the track or overarm at right angles to the guide fence. Turn the saw so that the blade is parallel to the guide fence. Then move the saw in or out until the correct distance between the guide fence and blade is obtained. Lock it in position. Set the depth of cut. Adjust the guard so that it is close to the work. Set the anti-kickback device so that the fingers rest firmly on the wood surface and hold it against the table. Check to make sure that the saw is rotating up and toward you.

Chapter 56

1. Two wheels mounted on a frame, a table, guides, a saw blade, and guards.
2. By the diameter of its wheels.
3. 1. Disconnect machine.
   2. Open upper and lower guard doors. Remove pin in table slot, and loosen vertical adjustment screw.
   3. Remove the old blade. If the blade is in one piece, pull the steel pin out of the slot in the table. Lower the upper wheel by turning the vertical adjustment wheel. Grasp the saw blade with both hands, lift it off of the upper and lower wheels. Coil it into three loops.
   4. Slip the new blade onto the upper and lower wheels with the teeth pointing downward. The guides should be back out of position. Tighten the vertical adjustment screw. Revolve the wheels by hand to see how the blade "rides." If the blade does not run in the center of the wheels, tilt the upper wheel with the tilt adjustment screw. The rear edge of the saw blade should be perpendicular to the table.
   5. Adjust the tension of the saw with the vertical adjustment screw. If the saw does not have a tensioning spring, the blade should bend $1/8$ to $1/4$ inch when pushed lightly on the side of the saw blade.
4. In front of the machine. Never stand to the right of the blade.

5. By making many relief cuts from the outside edge to within less than the thickness of the blade from the layout line.
6. A $1/8$-inch blade will cut down to about a $1/2$-inch circle. A $3/8$-inch blade will cut down to about a 2-inch circle.
7. Sawing stock to reduce its thickness.
8. Less stock is wasted.
9. By fastening a fence or pivot block to the table and proceeding in the same way as with a circular saw.

Chapter 57

1. Student will sketch a saw, locating its parts.
2. By the distance between the blade and the overarm, measured horizontally.
3. Power jig-saw blades, saber blades, jeweler's piercing blades.
4. Drill a relief hole in the center of the waste stock. If a jeweler's blade is to be used, remove the throat plate. After the blade is fastened in the lower chuck, put the stock over the blade. Fasten the other end of the blade to the plunger chuck. Then replace the throat plate. Adjust the guide to the correct height. Then make a circular cut from the relief hole to the layout line.
5. To make a simple inlay, first fasten two pieces of wood together in a pad. Nail then together with small brads at each corner. Drill a small hole at an inside corner of the design to start the blade. Now tilt the table of the saw 1 or 2 degrees. Make all necessary cuts, with the work always on the same side of the blade. Take the pad apart and assemble the design.

Chapter 58

1. Depth of cut scale, switch, base, out-feed or rear table, guard, in-feed or front table, fence, fence adjusting handle, front table adjusting hand wheel.
2. The length of the cutterhead knives.
3. The height of the in-feed table.
4. Refer to the chapter, where the safety precautions are detailed.
5. No.
6. With a try square.
7. Pushing the stock through the jointer too fast.
8. With a sliding T-bevel.
9. It will perform many operations not done on a conventional jointer.

Chapter 59

1. Shaping, sanding, routing, carving, mortising.
2. A spindle speed of 4,700 RPM.

3. A mortising attachment consists of a hollow, square mortising chisel in which an auger bit revolves. The chisel itself is ground to a sharp point at each corner. These points enter the wood just after the revolving bit. They cut the square opening after the bit has removed most of the stock.
4. By placing a collar of the correct diameter just above or below the cutter or by using a fence.
5. About 5,000 RPM.

Chapter 60
1. Stationary belt sander, stationary disk sander, narrow belt sander-grinder.
2. The abrasive paper must not be loose.
3. Safety precautions are detailed in the chapter.
4. Vertical, horizontal, or slant.
5. If the abrasive disk is worn, remove it. If the abrasive disk is attached with glue, soak it in hot water until loose. Then remove it with a putty knife. If rubber cement or stick cement was used, turn on the sander and hold the end of a hardwood stick against it. Move the stick back and forth to loosen the old adhesive. Be sure the metal disk is dry before mounting the new abrasive.
   To apply the new abrasive, hold the adhesive stick against the metal disk and move it back and forth. Make sure that there is a uniform coat of adhesive on the metal. Then turn off the power and carefully apply the abrasive. Let dry a short time. Clamp on a flat piece of wood to prevent wrinkles.

Chapter 61
1. A wood lathe is a powered device used in turning wood. Its main parts are a bed, headstock assembly, tailstock, tool rest, headstock spindle, and faceplate.
2. 1 inch gouge, $1/2$ inch gouge, 1 inch skew, $1\frac{1}{2}$ inch skew, roundnose, spear, parting tool.
3. Cutting and scraping.
4. Refer to the chapter, where safety precautions are discussed.
5. Tapping in with a wooden mallet to force the spur into the wood. With hardwood, it may be necessary to make two saw kerfs across the corners so that the wood will hold.
6. 3 inches thick.
7. If stock is rather large, adjust the lathe to its lowest speed. If stock is of medium diameter, adjust to medium speed. If stock is of small diameter, adjust to the highest speed.
8. The blade of a large gouge can be held in two ways. It can be grasped close to the cutting point with the hand underneath and the thumb over it. The forefinger then serves as a stop against the tool rest. Another way is to place your hand over the tool with your wrist bent at an angle to form the stop. Grasp the handle of the gouge in the other hand. Tilt it down and away from the direction in which the cut is to be made. Be sure to hold the tool tightly against the tool rest.
9. Its cutting edge is tapered.
10. Square the end that runs on the dead center with the parting tool or with the point of the skew chisel. Hold it so its side is flat on the tool rest.
    Measure the length of the cylinder from the squared end. Cut down with the toe of the skew chisel at this point. Hold the chisel so that this cut will be square to the cylinder. With the toe or heel of the skew chisel, make a series of sloping cuts against this square surface. Make the cut deeper gradually until only $1/4$ inch of the stock remains.
    Measure the length of the cylinder from the squared end. Cut down to this point from the parting tool until only $1/4$ inch of stock remains. This may then be cut through with the toe of the skew chisel.
    The end that runs on the dead center is squared with the point or toe of the skew chisel when its edge is held on the tool rest. The bevel of the chisel must be parallel to the end to make a square cut.
11. A parting tool, a small gouge, and a skew.
12. The heel.
13. A small skew.
14. Small articles such as bowls. Answers will vary.

Chapter 62
1. It can be used for installing and removing screws, cutting holes, sanding, grinding, and polishing.
2. Answers will vary. Safety rules are discussed in the chapter.
3. Answers will vary.

Chapter 63
1. Portable power (cutoff) saw, portable saber (bayonet) saw, reciprocating saw.
2. Because the portable saw cuts with the thrust upward.
3. Swing the guard out of the way. Place the front edge of the base plate on the work with the blade aligned over the line to be cut. Start the saw slowly and lower the blade into the stock.

4. The guide can be attached to the saw or a simple guide strip can be held against the edge of the stock and used as a guide for the saw.
5. Hold the tool at an angle, with the base resting on the surface. Turn on the power. Slowly lower the saw blade into the work until the blade cuts through the material. Then cut the opening.

Chapter 64
1. Collet-type chuck, cord strain reliever, motor safety disconnect, trigger switch, D-handle, housing, micrometer depth adjustment, guide knob, locking handle, sub-base.
2. Routing done without guides.
3. No.
4. Answers will vary.
5. To add a strip of inlay, first cut a groove the desired distance from the edge, using a left-hand spiral bit. Use a gauge to guide the router. Set the bit for the correct depth. This should equal the thickness of the inlaying material. The corners will be rounded and must be trimmed out with a chisel. The groove must be cut to the exact width of the inlay strip. Then cut the strip of inlay material with a miter corner. Fit each piece in to check the final design. Then apply glue to the back of the inlay and fasten it in the groove. Place a piece of wood over the inlay. Clamp it until the glue is dry.

Chapter 65
1. Answers will vary. Safety rules are discussed in the chapter.
2. Operate the portable belt sander as follows. Place the cord over your right shoulder or out of the way. Hold the machine firmly with both hands. Turn on the power. Lower the sander so that the heel touches the work first. Then move the sander back and forth in a straight line. Never allow the sander to stand still for any length of time. Always machine slowly and evenly.
3. When material is to be removed quickly.
4. To change a belt, first retract the front, free-turning roller of a belt sander. Then, after the new belt is on and the front roller returned to operating position, align the belt so it will not run off to one side during sanding.
5. Back-and-forth, or reciprocating; circular, or orbital.

Chapter 66
1. Lignin.
2. By counting the number of annual growth rings.

3. As hardwoods or softwoods; as having an open grain or a closed grain.
4. Coloring matter, annular rings, medullary rays, cross grain, wavy grain, knots, and other irregularities.
5. The ability of wood to absorb shock without permanent change in size.
6. Sulphur dioxide, ozone, ethylene.

Chapter 67
1. 758 million acres.
2. Government, 28 percent; private ownership, 60 percent; forest products industry, 12 percent.
3. 574,000.
4. 3, 5, 7, 9.
5. Veneer core: the core is made of thick wood veneer. Lumber core: the core is made of strips of lumber bonded together.
6. Manufactured board made from wood that has been reduced to the individual basic wood fibers. The fibers are compressed under heat and pressure to form hardboard.
7. Wood particles with resin binders.
8. Selective cutting: trees of a predetermined diameter are harvested. Clear cutting: All trees are harvested.
9. A plastic wedge is placed here to start and guide the fall of the tree.
10. Barking.
11. Cants.
12. Six months to two years.

Chapter 68
1. Pad seat, tight spring seat, overstuffed seat and back, sinuous (no-sag) springs.
2. Curled animal hair, Spanish moss, tow, shredded foam rubber.
3. Liquid latex.
4. Cushioned, feathered, square.
5. Make an open frame that will fit the main frame of the chair or bench. Apply the webbing. Tack a piece of burlap over the webbing. Cut a piece of upholstery cotton about 2 inches smaller in all directions than the frame. Apply the final covering.

Chapter 69
1. Solid and split.
2. White pine or mahogany.
3. The contraction of metal. Shrinkage results as the metal cools.
4. A slight taper on the vertical sides of a pattern. It makes it easier to draw the pattern from the mold.

5. A concave piece of material used to round off the sharp inside corners of patterns.

6. Drag and cope.

7. Sand is rammed around the pattern. The mold is vented. A bottom board is placed over the drag. Unit is turned over. Molding board is removed. Parting sand is sprinkled on. Cope is placed over drag. Riser pin is inserted. Sand is packed in the cope. Sprue and riser pins are removed. Sand is pierced with a needle. Cope is removed. Pattern is removed. Gate is cut from mold cavity. Cope is replaced. Molten metal is poured in sprue hole to fill mold. Sand is broken to remove casting.

8. Obtain a scale drawing with cross section shown in full size. Make a copy of the scale drawing that can be cut up. Cut out the cross sections, leaving them oversize. Cut templates to correct shape. Draw a center line on the work surface. Place section templates at right angles to center line at correct locations. Cut mahogany blocks of the correct size to fit between the sections. Glue the parts together. Work the wood down. Apply the finish.

9. A scale model is a small copy. A mock-up is a full-sized model built accurately to scale.

Chapter 70

1. Inputs—resources; process—what is done to the resources; output—the result of the system; feedback—reaction to the outputs.

2. People, materials, tools and machines, capital, information, time, energy.

3. Simplification of the product, standardization of each part, use of specialized machines, organization of workers.

4. Henry Ford. Interchangeability of parts, assembly line, division of labor, elimination of wasted motion.

5. Class may review product designs, and each member may select one to produce. Product can be given to a local charity or sold.

6. To hold work.

Chapter 71

1. Residential, commercial, industrial, and public works.

2. A mobile home is built on a chassis.

3. Western or platform frame.

4. A method of building high-rises or skyscrapers by pouring concrete into wood forms to which reinforcing rod has been added.

5. Use a scale of 1½ inches to the foot. Use scraps of lumber and basic woodworking tools. Use nails in proportion to the size of the scale model. Use standard house plans. Make shingles from sandpaper.

Chapter 72

1. Communication is the sharing of information, ideas, data, and instructions.

2. Computer, graphic, technical, optic, and audio/video.

3. The image is reproduced using powders and static electricity.

4. Graphic.

5. (Any 3) Dictating machine, fax machine, copy machine, telephone, computer, word processor, typewriter, robot, drawing equipment, scanner, radio, TV.

6. Individuals, society, and the environment.

Chapter 73

1. Transportation is the movement of goods and people from one place to another.

2. (Any 3) Balloon, dirigible, blimp, plane, rocket, space shuttle.

3. Because they can move slowly, remain stationary and fly low over the forests.

4. Fork lifts, bulldozers, excavators, trucks, and cranes.

5. Logs, lumber, and products are moved from one country to another using ships.

ANSWERS TO MATH SKILL EXERCISES AT END OF EACH SECTION

Section I. Width, 7″; height, 6½″.

Section II. Length of brace and bit, 390 mm, or 15.4 inches. Length of saw, 400 mm, or 15¾″.

Section III. End table: square feet in sides, 24′; area of top, 2081″.
Ping-pong table: plywood for top, 45 square feet; oak for legs, 0.47 board feet.

Section IV. Stain, 9.76; 10.
Filler, 15.61; 16.
Lacquer, 19.52; 20.
Square feet, 43.8′.

Section V. 1. 7225.7 fpm.
2. 9032.1 fpm.
3. 117.8 fpm.
4. 6178.5 fpm.

Section VI. Circumference, 56.5″; height, 7.3 m.

Section VII. Width of top, 27⅛″; length of top, 81″; overhang, 1½″.
Width of house itself, 31′5″; width of house including garage, 47′2″; square feet in master bedroom, 152′4″; concrete, 84 cu ft.

Student Workbook Answer Key

Unit 1
1. T
2. input
3. processing
4. plotter
5. binary
6. access
7. read
8. software
9. programmers
10. numerical
11. feedback
12. robot
13. radiation
14. T
15. T
16. receiver
17. printer
18. bit
19. byte
20. hardware
21. design
22. manufacturing
23. T
24. manipulators

Unit 2
1. sides
2. T
3. dressed
4. F
5. F
6. F
7. b
8. c
9. e
10. f
11. a
12. d
13. T
14. kiln
15. 12
16. structural
17. F
18. FAS
19. Common
20. 45
21. c
22. T
23. good

24. T
25. $2' \times 12'$
26. adhesives
27. T
28. 3/4 inch
29. oriented
30. molding
31. b
32. e
33. d
34. c
35. a
36. African
37. T
38. 300
39. black
40. c
41. gum
42. Bird's-eye
43. Willow
44. b

Unit 3
1. function
2. d
3. secondary
4. tertiary
5. informal
6. a
7. pictorial
8. T
9. 120
10. T
11. F
12. exploded
13. visible outline
14. invisible outline
15. center line
16. extension line
17. dimension line
18. F
19. dual
20. perspective
21. isometric
22. cabinet
23. isometric
24. materials
25. stock-cutting
26. 12
27. square

28. linear
29. c
30. 12
31. b
32. T

Unit 4
1. metric
2. equator
3. d
4. F
5. c
6. kilogram
7. 39.37
8. 25.4
9. b
10. millimetre
11. 1/25
12. 1,000
13. centimetres
14. 1-foot bench rule
15. zigzag rule
16. combination square
17. siding T-bevel
18. sloyd knife
19. steel tape
20. carpenter's framing square
21. scratch awl
22. b
23. F
24. pencil
25. vise
26. vise
27. c
28. b
29. F

Unit 5
1. T
2. apron
3. eye
4. Safety
5. T
6. F
7. F
8. T
9. F
10. pledge
11. T
12. Outlook

13. T
14. technicians
15. b
16. d
17. helper
18. finish
19. b
20. T
21. forester
22. architects
23. T
24. b
25. two
26. T

Unit 6
1. crosscut
2. ripsaw
3. b
4. T
5. T
6. chisel
7. c
8. T
9. T
10. F
11. F
12. 60
13. crosscut
14. ripsaw
15. T
16. F
17. F
18. six
19. up
20. wedge
21. T

Unit 7
1. F
2. handle
3. lateral adjusting lever
4. heel
5. adjusting nut
6. frog
7. lever cap
8. bottom
9. body
10. toe
11. knob
12. plane iron and plane iron cap
13. hand
14. jack
15. smooth
16. fore (jointer)

17. fore (jointer)
18. c
19. a
20. d
21. b
22. e
23. breaker
24. c
25. e
26. b
27. f
28. a
29. d
30. F
31. F
32. crook
33. cup
34. wind (twist)
35. T
36. F
37. F
38. T
39. F
40. side
41. side
42. long
43. b
44. c
45. T
46. T
47. spur
48. F
49. plate
50. finger rest knob
51. cam
52. lever cap
53. cutter
54. lateral adjusting lever
55. adjusting nut
56. bottom
57. F
58. F
59. F
60. T
61. $^{1}/_{32}$
62. F
63. F
64. block
65. jumping

Unit 8
1. F
2. hook
3. F
4. F

5. F
6. T
7. F
8. dovetail
9. teeth
10. adhesive
11. c
12. b
13. e
14. d
15. g
16. h
17. f
18. a
19. F
20. c
21. c
22. T
23. T
24. F
25. C-clamp
26. hand screw
27. spring screw
28. cabinet clamp (bar clamp)
29. speed bar clamps
30. 15
31. dowels
32. single
33. T
34. opposite
35. T
36. T
37. chisel
38. F
39. six
40. T
41. cornering

Unit 9
1. T
2. F
3. dividers
4. dividers
5. pencil compass
6. half
7. trammel
8. string
9. octagon
10. hexagon
11. b
12. c
13. ellipse
14. T
15. $^{1}/_{4}$
16. template

17. T
18. ellipse
19. T
20. coping
21. compass
22. T
23. d
24. b
25. T
26. T
27. T
28. wax
29. T
30. F
31. T
32. F
33. F
34. T
35. 8
36. spokeshave
37. drawknife
38. cabinet file
39. rasp
40. Surform® tool
41. F
42. F
43. vise
44. chatter
45. deep
46. F
47. F
48. F
49. F
50. T
51. F
52. vise
53. F
54. F
55. F
56. F
57. F
58. card
59. T
60. c
61. rasp
62. F
63. T
64. router
65. d
66. F
67. T
68. T

Unit 10
1. chamfer

2. F
3. three
4. a
5. T
6. stop
7. through
8. stop
9. T
10. b
11. T
12. plane
13. protractor
14. straight
15. F
16. taper
17. T
18. F
19. plane
20. T
21. F
22. curved
23. mallet
24. behind
25. tang
26. socket
27. socket
28. tang
29. b
30. a
31. d
32. c
33. F
34. F
35. F
36. T
37. T
38. flat
39. F
40. T
41. across
42. flat
43. F
44. F
45. T
46. T
47. T
48. T
49. T
50. F
51. T
52. mallet
53. c
54. b
55. a
56. e

57. d
58. T
59. wood
60. PEG
61. three
62. dry
63. T
64. F
65. skew
66. T
67. V
68. T
69. F
70. T

Unit 11
1. oak
2. three
3. boiling
4. 25
5. 2
6. ten
7. F
8. C-clamps
9. T
10. twenty-four
11. F
12. right
13. T
14. T
15. F
16. birch
17. T
18. T
19. waxed
20. twenty-four
21. mineral
22. wax

Unit 12
1. b
2. c
3. d
4. a
5. tang
6. c
7. $5/16$
8. d
9. b
10. 1
11. T
12. Forstner
13. speed (flat)
14. a
15. brace

16. c
17. a
18. e
19. d
20. b
21. brace
22. ratchet
23. awl
24. T
25. T
26. T
27. gauge
28. T-bevel
29. b
30. F
31. $1/4$
32. f
33. b
34. a
35. e
36. c
37. d
38. body
39. shank
40. flute
41. land
42. hand drill
43. hand
44. 3
45. bit
46. T-bevel
47. T
48. auger

Unit 13
1. 30
2. try
3. F
4. two and one-half
5. T
6. F
7. $1/16$
8. honed (whetted)
9. carbide
10. F
11. machine
12. c
13. T
14. T
15. F
16. T
17. F
18. c
19. file
20. oilstone

21. d
22. T
23. burnishing
24. T
25. F
26. spur
27. solvent
28. speed
29. F
30. T
31. T
32. chisels
33. taper

Unit 14
1. c
2. a
3. b
4. corner
5. T
6. F
7. T
8. T
9. edge
10. b
11. 1
12. T
13. F
14. F
15. $1/8$
16. jig
17. square
18. bevel
19. dowels
20. T
21. b
22. a
23. rabbet
24. T
25. T
26. b
27. two-thirds
28. c
29. T
30. T
31. T
32. F
33. dado
34. T
35. one-half
36. grain
37. T
38. F
39. rabbet
40. c

41. rabbet
42. F
43. a
44. b
45. blind

Unit 15
1. edge cross lap
2. half lap
3. end lap
4. middle lap
5. F
6. cross
7. cross
8. chisel
9. b
10. plane
11. T
12. F
13. d
14. T
15. d
16. splines
17. corner
18. T
19. T
20. rabbet
21. T
22. finishing
23. F
24. blind
25. T
26. legs
27. one-half
28. $3/4$
29. F
30. T
31. a
32. auger
33. width
34. gauge
35. chisel
36. F
37. crosscut
38. T
39. T
40. adhesives

Unit 16
1. edge
2. rabbet
3. dado
4. block
5. F
6. F

7. T
8. F
9. F
10. d
11. groove
12. smaller
13. dado
14. F
15. T
16. F
17. F
18. F
19. slide
20. c
21. T
22. F
23. F
24. F
25. bevel
26. plane
27. a

Unit 17
1. poll
2. neck
3. wedges
4. head
5. claw
6. handle
7. adze eye
8. check
9. face
10. set
11. ripping
12. common
13. box
14. finishing
15. casing
16. galvanized
17. 60
18. T
19. 4½
20. a
21. d
22. escutcheon
23. T
24. finishing
25. flat
26. oval
27. duplex
28. spikes
29. F
30. head
31. split
32. ¹/₁₆

33. a
34. F
35. toenailing
36. T
37. tip
38. blade
39. ferrule
40. handle
41. head
42. three
43. F
44. Phillips
45. offset
46. F
47. pilot
48. soap
49. aluminum
50. T
51. pilot
52. Wire
53. 24
54. T
55. T
56. T
57. T
58. b
59. F
60. T
61. F
62. c
63. flush (even)
64. 82
65. brace
66. drill press
67. F
68. F
69. plug
70. screwdriver
71. brace

Unit 18
1. T
2. T
3. F
4. d
5. hand scraper
6. cabinet scraper
7. T
8. F
9. F
10. F
11. F
12. quartz
13. F
14. F

15. abrasive
16. felt
17. T
18. F
19. T
20. T
21. T
22. T
23. F
24. T
25. jig
26. softwood
27. T
28. square
29. parallel (square)
30. a
31. c
32. b
33. f
34. d
35. e
36. T
37. F
38. T
39. F
40. F
41. F
42. F
43. 24
44. flat
45. recess (gain)
46. T
47. c
48. rails
49. chisel
50. F
51. lip
52. overlay
53. T
54. mending
55. flat corner
56. bent corner
57. T-plate
58. mending
59. center

Unit 19
1. miter
2. cut
3. b
4. c
5. a
6. d
7. c
8. rotary

9. flat sliced
10. half round
11. quartered
12. rotary cut
13. F
14. $\frac{1}{28}$
15. flitch
16. T
17. vertical butt (horizontal bookleaf)
18. slip
19. book
20. random
21. T
22. F
23. F
24. T
25. pressure
26. iron
27. cement
28. F
29. 30
30. T
31. T
32. T
33. c
34. iron
35. T
36. laminate
37. carbide
38. F
39. F
40. F
41. F
42. brittle
43. F
44. F
45. T
46. crack
47. F
48. T
49. F
50. F
51. T
52. F
53. T
54. file
55. b
56. c
57. a
58. b
59. d

Unit 20
1. b

2. d
3. e
4. f
5. g
6. c
7. a
8. T
9. T
10. b
11. d
12. f
13. a
14. c
15. e
16. hog
17. nylon
18. T
19. F
20. F
21. F
22. T
23. F
24. T
25. F
26. F
27. F
28. lacquer thinner
29. turpentine
30. alcohol
31. turpentine
32. turpentine
33. tip
34. bristles
35. ferrule
36. handle
37. setting
38. divider
39. f
40. b
41. a
42. h
43. g
44. d
45. c
46. e
47. i
48. F
49. oil
50. aluminum
51. F
52. tack
53. F
54. iron
55. 15
56. putty

57. wool
58. coater
59. F
60. T
61. T
62. b
63. T
64. T
65. F
66. brush
67. a
68. F
69. T
70. 24
71. shellac
72. T
73. T
74. T
75. pigment (tinting color)
76. T
77. T
78. T
79. F
80. F
81. T
82. T
83. shellac
84. bleeding
85. brush
86. F
87. F
88. T
89. alcohol
90. F

Unit 21
1. lac
2. b
3. alcohol
4. T
5. shellac
6. F
7. F
8. T
9. 4
10. wool
11. F
12. sandpaper
13. pumice
14. rottenstone
15. benzine
16. F
17. alcohol
18. F
19. spar

20. T
21. F
22. F
23. tack
24. F
25. turpentine
26. F
27. F
28. T
29. T
30. turpentine
31. 24
32. F
33. T
34. T
35. T
36. T
37. 8
38. penetrating
39. b
40. a
41. c
42. wax
43. F
44. 30
45. three
46. F
47. F
48. F
49. T
50. water
51. shellac
52. F
53. T
54. F
55. T
56. F
57. aerosol
58. respirator
59. T
60. 8
61. F
62. perpendicular
63. 5
64. lacquer

Unit 22
1. F
2. point
3. pigment
4. latex
5. water
6. flat
7. spirits
8. T

9. T
10. F
11. T
12. F
13. T
14. T
15. T
16. F
17. glaze
18. paint
19. F
20. F
21. brush
22. F
23. overnight
24. T
25. F
26. 15
27. F
28. highlighted
29. T
30. T
31. T
32. varnish

Unit 23
1. F
2. T
3. T
4. F
5. F
6. brush
7. T
8. d
9. T
10. T
11. surfacer
12. c
13. a
14. cutting feed selector handle
15. switch
16. table
17. elevating hand wheel
18. F
19. outfeed roll
20. pressure bar
21. gib
22. cutterhead
23. knife
24. chip breaker
25. infeed roll
26. T
27. T
28. T
29. jointer

30. c
31. T

Unit 24
1. p
2. e
3. t
4. i
5. c
6. q
7. l
8. d
9. b
10. g
11. n
12. k
13. o
14. j
15. f
16. r
17. s
18. a
19. m
20. h
21. c
22. saw-raising
23. crosscut
24. rip
25. standard combination
26. combination
27. splitter
28. F
29. a
30. push
31. F
32. T
33. T
34. T
35. arbor
36. T
37. blade
38. a
39. stop
40. block
41. crosscutting
42. gauge
43. blade
44. F
45. blade
46. c
47. dado
48. F
49. shoulder
50. c
51. d

52. dado head
53. dado
54. T
55. adjustable
56. ³/₄
57. jig
58. F
59. b
60. m
61. f
62. h
63. e
64. a
65. k
66. l
67. c
68. j
69. d
70. g
71. i
72. cutoff
73. T
74. crosscutting
75. ripping
76. blades
77. track
78. 360
79. 90
80. b
81. c
82. a
83. T
84. F
85. F
86. right
87. b
88. ¹/₈
89. arm (track)
90. T
91. arm (track)
92. a
93. F
94. T
95. T

Unit 25
1. wheels
2. 2
3. T
4. T
5. b
6. 2
7. b
8. a
9. c

10. e
11. d
12. f
13. h
14. g
15. backtracking
16. T
17. waste
18. T
19. ¹/₄
20. thinner
21. T
22. relief
23. jig
24. thickness
25. circular
26. gauge
27. tilting
28. base
29. over arm
30. motor
31. guide assembly
32. tension sleeve
33. guide post
34. upper chuck
35. table
36. hold down
37. 4-step cone pulley
38. T
39. d
40. T
41. jeweler's
42. saber
43. T
44. down
45. 5
46. F
47. support
48. light
49. F
50. T
51. T
52. b
53. T
54. relief
55. plunger
56. bevel
57. marquetry

Unit 26
1. e
2. h
3. b
4. c
5. g

6. j
7. a
8. d
9. f
10. i
11. a
12. T
13. infeed
14. F
15. F
16. snipe
17. T
18. b
19. push
20. F
21. cutterhead
22. c
23. T
24. F
25. F
26. F
27. right
28. ripples
29. d
30. rabbet
31. Uniplane®
32. d
33. b
34. p
35. m
36. j
37. f
38. o
39. r
40. h
41. n
42. a
43. c
44. e
45. g
46. i
47. k
48. l
49. q
50. s
51. T
52. T
53. 90
54. miter
55. T
56. T
57. T
58. T
59. twist drill
60. space bit

61. spur machine bit
62. multispur machine bit
63. Forstner bit
64. expansive bit
65. countersink
66. F
67. mortising
68. 4,700
69. T
70. adapter
71. collar
72. 5,000
73. T
74. drum
75. belt
76. lock
77. T
78. push
79. abrasive
80. disc

Unit 27
1. F
2. speed control hand wheel
3. hand wheel and index
4. indexing pin
5. headstock
6. switch
7. headstock spindle
8. tool support base
9. calibrated tool support
10. tailstock locking clamp
11. spindle
12. spindle lock
13. hand wheel
14. tailstock
15. bed
16. steel cabinet
17. T
18. bed
19. T
20. spur
21. spur (live center)
22. T
23. scraping
24. e
25. c
26. f
27. b
28. a
29. d
30. rule
31. dividers
32. outside caliper
33. inside caliper

34. hermaphrodite caliper
35. cutting
36. scraping
37. T
38. cutting
39. scraping
40. b
41. T
42. F
43. 1
44. T
45. 1/8
46. F
47. T
48. two
49. 1/8
50. skew
51. F
52. cutting
53. scraping
54. plane
55. parting
56. skew
57. c
58. T
59. F
60. F
61. skew
62. F
63. roundnose
64. T
65. T
66. duplicator
67. T
68. screw center
69. standard
70. F
71. screws
72. T
73. live
74. F
75. F
76. a
77. chisel
78. chuck
79. French
80. T

Unit 28
1. twist
2. key
3. awl
4. jig
5. cutoff
6. F

7. power CIRCULAR SAW
8. portable saber saw
9. reciprocating
10. T
11. blade
12. T
13. 10
14. down
15. T
16. d
17. T
18. T
19. F
20. c
21. T
22. T
23. 2
24. F
25. T
26. T
27. rip
28. b
29. hole
30. F
31. collet
32. nut
33. base
34. clockwise
35. T
36. T
37. straight
38. chamfer
39. V-groove
40. cove
41. rabbet
42. T
43. T
44. F
45. pilot
46. T
47. spiral
48. T
49. chisel
50. F
51. inlaying
52. F
53. orbital
54. straight-line
55. T
56. T
57. T
58. F

Unit 29
1. deciduous

2. coniferous
3. grain
4. cellulose
5. springwood
6. summerwood
7. growth
8. a
9. cambium
10. fiber-saturation
11. dry
12. a
13. water
14. 1.0
15. bending
16. resilience
17. pollution
18. ozone
19. oxygen
20. a
21. T
22. cambium
23. phloem
24. bark
25. sapwood
26. heartwood
27. pith
28. medullary ray
29. clear-cutting
30. d
31. bucking
32. barking
33. c
34. kilns
35. d
36. T
37. a
38. core
39. veneer
40. T
41. particle
42. 20
43. wood

Unit 30
1. T
2. webbing
3. ½
4. T
5. gimp
6. burlap
7. F
8. cement
9. T
10. T
11. c

12. a
13. e
14. f
15. b
16. d
17. F
18. T
19. F
20. F
21. F
22. T
23. no-sag
24. T
25. flax
26. stretcher

Unit 31
1. c
2. T
3. split
4. T
5. sand
6. plywood
7. T
8. b
9. F
10. F
11. d
12. leather
13. shellac
14. fillet
15. T
16. flask
17. cope
18. drag
19. sand
20. T
21. bottom
22. parting
23. a
24. riser
25. F
26. riser
27. needle
28. pattern
29. gate
30. sprue
31. T
32. cope
33. mock-up
34. template
35. scale
36. longitudinal
37. T
38. cope

39. sprue pin
40. riser pin
41. pattern
42. drag
43. flask
44. bottom board

Unit 32
1. T
2. standardization
3. a
4. capital
5. human
6. d
7. a
8. b
9. e
10. c
11. jig
12. fixture
13. template
14. quality
15. Whitney
16. personnel
17. sectional
18. chassis
19. nine
20. 14
21. elevations
22. 10
23. permits
24. footings
25. foundation
26. 8
27. waterproof
28. T
29. sill
30. T
31. platform (western)
32. joists
33. joists
34. 24
35. T
36. T
37. T
38. c
39. T
40. sheathing
41. T
42. subfloor
43. T
44. F
45. plate
46. plywood
47. F

48. T
49. F
50. F
51. F
52. c
53. T
54. T
55. beams or timbers
56. b
57. resources
58. F
59. capital
60. F
61. computers

Unit 33
1. ideas
2. c
3. F
4. T
5. T
6. F
7. c
8. T
9. F
10. T
11. c
12. T
13. T
14. d
15. F
16. T
17. F
18. T
19. universal
20. b
21. T
22. T
23. fax
24. F
25. glass
26. CAD
27. F
28. T
29. architect
30. electronic services
31. people
32. cost
33. space
34. c
35. marine
36. d
37. T
38. advertising
39. F
40. T
41. upward
42. 18
43. cargo
44. ties
45. crane
46. T
47. excavator
48. conveyor
49. freighters

ANSWERS TO SCIENCE ACTIVITIES IN THE STUDENT WORKBOOK

Activity I: Determining Wood Density

Related science: chemistry, physics
Hints: A dieter's food scale with 100-gram markings can be used if a scientific scale is not available. Blocks should have rectangular or square faces so that volume is easy to calculate. The greater the variety, the better. The same kind of wood may vary in density, depending on the sample; errors in calculation or differences in block dimensions may also cause variances. The following table gives a range of densities for several common woods.

Wood	Density (cu. cm)	Wood	Density (cu. cm)
ash	0.65-0.85	maple	0.62-0.72
balsa	0.11-0.14	pine (white)	0.35-0.50
birch	0.51-0.77	pine (yellow)	0.37-0.60
cedar	0.49-0.57	poplar	0.35-0.50
cherry	0.70-0.90	spruce	0.48-0.70
ebony	1.11-1.33	teak	0.66-0.88
mahogany	0.66-0.85	walnut	0.64-0.70

Activity II: How Muscles Work

Related science: human anatomy and physiology
Answers: (1) Arm and shoulder because more muscles are involved. (2) Whichever is the student's dominant hand will exert more force because that hand is used more. (3) When sawing, only movement is required; the saw's weight supplies the force; during planing, the operator must supply the force; planing causes more fibers to contract.

Activity III: Hardness of Abrasives

Related science: geology (mineralogy)
Hints: Hardness is one of the properties geologists use to identify a mineral. The Mohs hardness numbers for minerals students may recognize include: fool's gold (6.3); opal (4-6); graphite in lead pencils (0.5-1); asbestos (5); and mica (2.5).
Answers: (1) The Mohs number for garnet is a range from 6.5 to 7. (4) Most woods must have a hardness lower than that of quartz or garnet because abrasives must be harder than the wood they are used to sand.

Activity IV: Solutions

Related science: chemistry
Hints: Why a solvent dissolves one substance and not another is still not understood; generally, a solvent dissolves things that are chemically similar. Be sure the mineral spirits are disposed of properly after the experiment.
Answer: The mothball and linseed oil will dissolve in the mineral spirits; the sugar and alcohol will dissolve in the water; the steel wool will dissolve in neither.

Activity V: Work and Power

Related science: physics
Hints: A stepstool may be used instead of stairs. Have students measure the time required to step up and down 20-30 times; then divide by 2 to find the time in seconds (half is taken in stepping down). The total height is then the number of steps up multiplied by the height of the stool.
Answers: (4) Both work and power increase if a 20-lb. load is added. (5) Power increases if the student does the work faster, but work remains the same.

Activity VI: Leaf Structure and Tree Growth

Related science: botany, plant physiology
Hints: One square inch of the underside of a deciduous leaf can contain 100,000 or more stomata. Students will also observe fibrovascular bundles. On the top of the leaf they will see a pattern of epidermal cells and veins.
Answers: (1) On the underside. (2) They should see differences in size and number. (3) The leaf covered with petroleum jelly will not wilt as quickly because water cannot escape. (4) If pollutants prevent the stomata from functioning, photosynthesis cannot take place, roots do not bring in more water and minerals, and the tree will sicken and die.

Activity VII: Forces in Wood Framing

Related science: physics
Answers: (1) The downward force of the weight exceeded the upward force of the blocks. (2) It would have broken. (3) The downward force was distributed among more supports and the yardstick no longer sagged. (4) Increased them. (5) Joist; studs. (6) The force exerted by the load; the strength of the supports; the cost of supports and labor needed to install them; building codes.

ANSWERS TO MATH ACTIVITIES IN THE STUDENT WORKBOOK

Activity I-1: Using the Binary System

```
  54 = 110110
 127 = 1111111
 288 = 100100000
 382 = 101111110
 464 = 111010000
 693 = 1010110101
 765 = 1011111101
 812 = 1100101100
 907 = 1110001011
1023 = 1111111111
```

1. 10000 (10 + 6 = 16)
2. 1001 (1 + 8 = 9)
3. 10111 (8 + 15 = 23)
4. 11001 (12 + 13 = 25)
5. 11110 (14 + 16 = 30)
6. 26 (1110 + 1100 = 11010)
7. 21 (110 + 1111 = 10101)
8. 32 (10000 + 10000 = 100000)
9. 17 (1000 + 1001 = 10001)

Activity II-1: Using the Metric System

1. 5.08
2. 1.37
3. 301.75
4. 7.62
5. .615
6. .0945
7. 1.85
8. 3.609
9. .951
10. 3.66

Activity II-2: Using a Ruler

1. 16
2. 10; millimetre
3. 2.5
4. 25
5. 100
6. 9; 90
7. 1.5
8. $3/8$
9. 1,503

Activity III-1: Wood Screw Sizes

1. .312
2. 3″
3. #9 or #10
4. 16
5. .091
6. Hard wood; $1/32$
7. $11/64$; $6/32$ or $3/16$
8. $1/64$
9. 1
10. #18; 4.5

Activity III-2: Fractions and Decimals

1. .75
2. .125
3. .0625
4. .093
5. .222
6. .571
7. .833

8. .172
9. $^{11}/_{16}$
10. $^{1}/_{8}$
11. $^{23}/_{30}$
12. $^{7}/_{12}$
13. $1^{3}/_{8}$
14. $^{5}/_{16}$
15. 1
16. $2^{1}/_{2}$
17. $10^{9}/_{20}$
18. $^{1}/_{16}$
19. 6
20. $2^{4}/_{5}$
21. $^{1}/_{5}$
22. $^{4}/_{9}$
23. $^{1}/_{32}$
24. $^{11}/_{24}$
25. $^{1}/_{8}$
26. $2^{7}/_{12}$
27. $^{7}/_{16}$
28. $1^{9}/_{10}$

Activity IV-1: Finishing Coverage

1. a. 1110
   b. 666
   c. 540
   d. 540
2. 19.83; number of square feet to be finished
3. a. 17.65
   b. 11.34
   c. 8.82
4. 32.16
5. 25,200

Activity V-1: Reading a Table

1. 6″ to 8″
2. 6″
3. over 10″
4. Finishing; roughing to size
5. 1200 RPM
6. Finishing
7. Roughing requires a slower cut for accuracy
8. 9
9. 1800 RPM
10. 3 times faster

Activity V-2: Costs of Electricity

1. a. 154
   b. 142,450
   c. 142.45
   d. $19.94
   e. $.91; $239.28
2. a. 60
   b. 66,000
   c. 66; 792
   d. $5.94
   e. $.396; $71.28

Activity VI-1: Figuring Percentages

1. 32
2. 19
3. 9
4. 120
5. 360
6. 100
7. 12.5%
8. 350%
9. 90%
10. 35%

Activity VII-1: Indirect Measurement

1. Answers will vary. Height of the house in the drawing is 29 feet.
2. Answers will vary. Height of the tree in the drawing is 30 feet.
3. Answers will vary.

Activity VII-2: Reading a Drawing

1. 2″
2. 275; 1.91
3. 11″
4. $1^{1}/_{2}$″
5. $^{1}/_{4}$″
6. $^{1}/_{2}$″; $^{1}/_{2}$″
7. The end is shorter so it can fit within the sides properly.

Progress Chart

	Student's Name	Assignment														
		1	2	3	4	5	6	7	8	9	10	11	12	13	14	15
1																
2																
3																
4																
5																
6																
7																
8																
9																
10																
11																
12																
13																
14																
15																
16																
17																
18																
19																
20																
21																
22																
23																
24																
25																
26																
27																
28																

Projects

Project 1. Salad Server Set

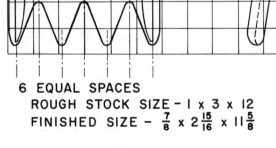

Bill of Materials

1 piece light-colored hardwood, 3″ x ⅞″ x 24″
1 piece dark-colored hardwood, 4″ x ¼″ x 4½″
8″ of ⅜″ dowel.

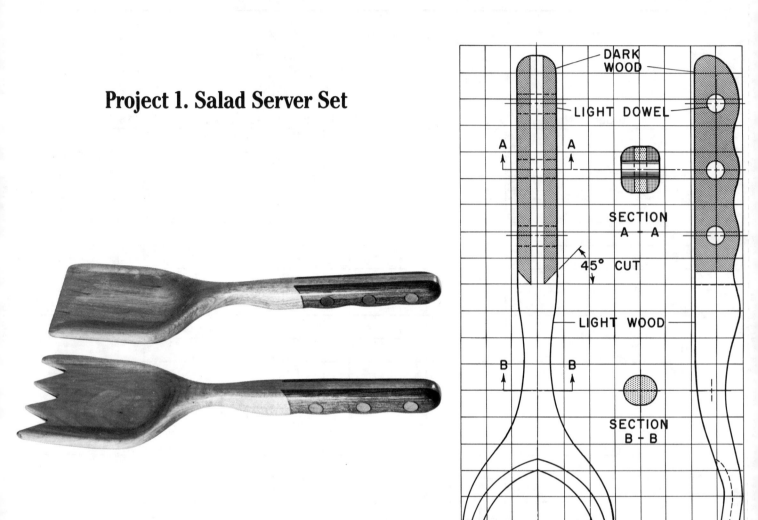

DARK WOOD

LIGHT DOWEL

A   A

SECTION
A - A

45° CUT

LIGHT WOOD

B   B

SECTION
B - B

SECTION
C - C

6 EQUAL SPACES
ROUGH STOCK SIZE - 1 x 3 x 12
FINISHED SIZE - $\frac{7}{8}$ x 2$\frac{15}{16}$ x 11$\frac{5}{8}$

Project 2. Salt and Pepper Shaker Set

NO. 50 DRILL

USE NO. 55 DRILL

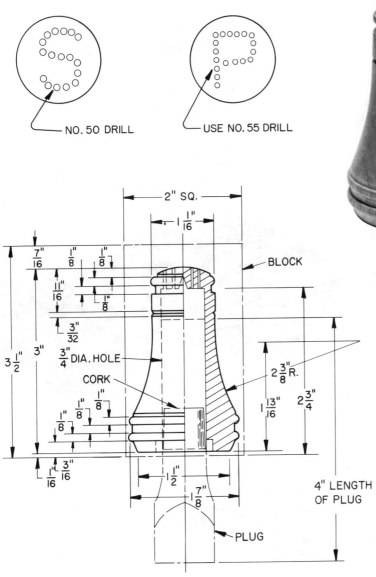

2" SQ.

$1\frac{1}{16}$"

BLOCK

$\frac{7}{16}$" $\frac{1}{8}$" $\frac{1}{8}$"

$\frac{11}{16}$" $\frac{1}{8}$"

$\frac{3}{32}$"

$3\frac{1}{2}$"   3" $\frac{3}{4}$" DIA. HOLE

CORK

$\frac{1}{8}$" $\frac{1}{8}$" $\frac{1}{8}$"

$\frac{1}{8}$"

$2\frac{3}{8}$"R.

$1\frac{13}{16}$" $2\frac{3}{4}$"

$\frac{1}{16}$" $\frac{3}{16}$"

$1\frac{1}{2}$"

$1\frac{7}{8}$"

PLUG

4" LENGTH
OF PLUG

Bill of Materials

STOCK: Birch, Mahogany, or Maple Important: All dimensions listed below are FINISHED size.					
No. of Pieces	Part Name	Thick- ness	Width	Length	Material
2	Shakers	2"	2"	3½"	Birch, Mahogany, or Maple
1 2	Plug Corks	1" ¾" D.	1"	4"	Hardwood

Project 3. Server Tray

Plan of Procedure

1. Cut all pieces to size on circular saw.
2. Round edges of base on wood shaper or with file and sandpaper.
3. By measurement, lay out angles on side, end, and center pieces. Set circular saw miter gage to proper angle and cut ends of sides and end pieces.
4. Set saw arbor to 15-degree angle and cut angle on top and bottom edges of side and end pieces so that bottom edges will fit flush on base and top edges will be level.
5. Set saw arbor to 5-degree angle and cut angle on ends of side pieces to fit squarely against side pieces.
6. Lay out handle. Drill ⅜-inch hole at each end of finger grip and cut out on jig saw.
7. Smooth all pieces with sandpaper.
8. Assemble with glue and wire brads. Drill nail holes slightly smaller than brads to prevent splitting the wood. It may be necessary to shorten length of handle slightly to fit in ends of tray.
9. Set brads. Fill holes.
10. Thoroughly soften all edges and finish sand entire project.
11. Apply antique pine finish.

Bill of Materials

No. of Pieces	Part Name	Thick-ness	Width	Length
	STOCK: Pine Important: All dimensions listed below are FINISHED size.			
1	Base	⁵⁄₁₆″	3⅛″	4⅞″
2	Sides	³⁄₁₆″	1⁷⁄₁₆″	5½″
2	Ends	³⁄₁₆″	1⁷⁄₁₆″	3⅜″
1	Handle	³⁄₁₆″	1⅝″	5⅛″

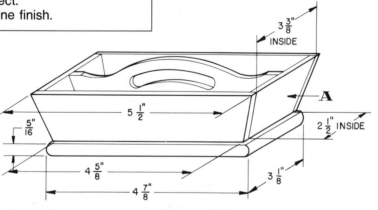

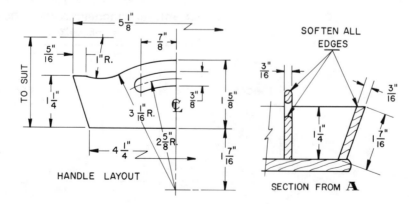

HANDLE LAYOUT

SECTION FROM **A**

58

Project 4. Planter/Spoon Rack

Plan of Procedure

1. Cut out all pieces to size on circular saw.
2. Lay out irregular design on back and cut out on jig saw.
3. Lay out holes in spoon racks. Drill ¼-inch holes in waste areas and cut out on jig saw.
4. Lay out corner joints on planter side and ends and cut out on circular saw.
5. Thoroughly soften edges of back and spoon racks. Smooth all pieces with sandpaper.
6. Glue up front and two end pieces of planter.
7. Fit, glue, and nail bottom to front and sides. Set nails.
8. Lay out, drill, and countersink screw shank holes. Drill anchor holes. Drill mounting holes in back.
9. Attach spoon racks and planter box to back with No. 4 F. H. wood screws.
10. Fill nail holes and finish sand entire project.
11. Apply antique pine finish.
12. Lay out, bend, and solder planter lining. Paint dark green if galvanized sheet steel is used.

Bill of Materials

No. of Pieces	Part Name	Thick-ness	Width	Length
1	Back	⅜"	12"	20"
1	Front	⅜"	4½"	12"
2	Ends	⅜"	4½"	3⅝"
1	Bottom	⅜"	3¼"	11¼"
2	Spoon Racks	⅜"	1"	12"
10	No. 4 x 1¼" F. H. Wood Screws			
8	No. 4 x 1" F. H. Wood Screws			
1	Planter Lining No. 26 ga. (Galv. sheet steel or copper.)		11⅞"	19⅞"
10	No. 18 x 1¼" Wire Brads			

STOCK: Pine
Important: All dimensions listed below are FINISHED size.

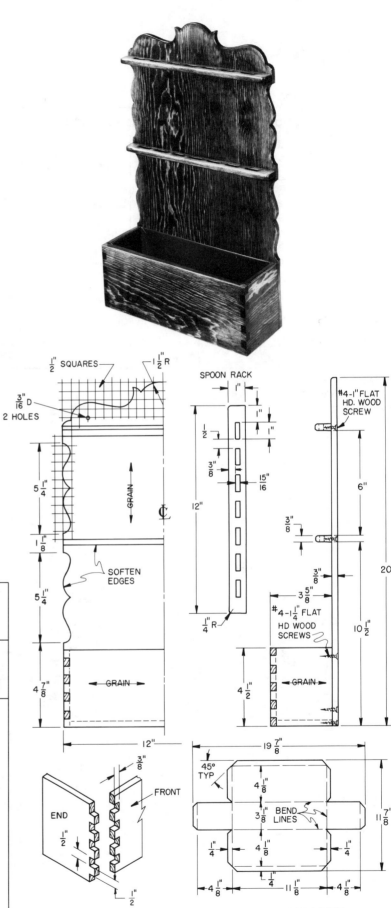

SPOON RACK

PLANTER LINING LAYOUT

Project 5. Sewing Box

Bill of Materials

No. of Pieces	Thickness	Width	Length	Description	Kind of Wood
**Important: All dimensions listed below are FINISHED size.**					
1	½"	1⅝"	9¼"	Handle	Pine
2	⅜"	5⅜"	9¼"	Sides	Pine
2	⅜"	7⅛"	7³⁄₁₆"	Ends	Pine
1	⅜"	2½"	10¼"	Top	Pine
2	⅜"	4¼"	10¼"	Lids	Pine
1	⅜"	4¾"	8½"	Bottom	Pine
4				1" Brass Butt Hinges	
2				No. 6 x ¾" F.H. Wood Screws	
2				No. 6 x 1¼" F.H. Wood Screws	
2				No. 18 x 1" Wire Brads	

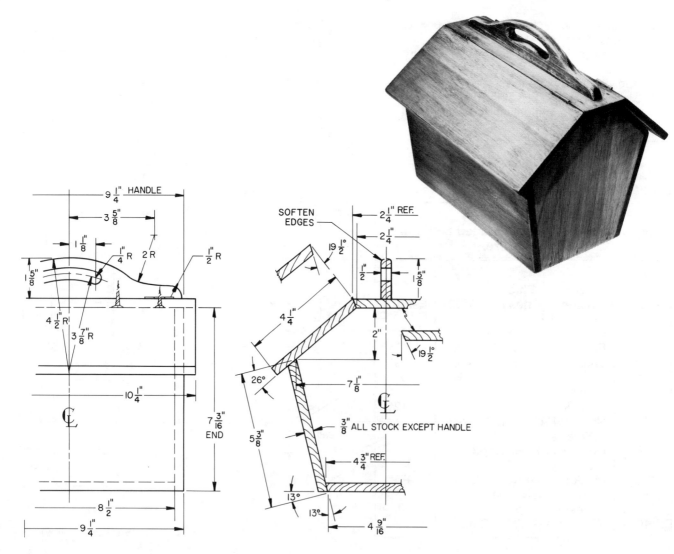

Project 6. Lamp

Bill of Materials

No. of Pieces	Part Name	Thick-ness	Width	Length
4	Column Stock	1¾"	5¼"	15"
4	Column Stock	¾"	2¾"	15"
1	Base	¾"	7¼"	7¼"
1	Cap	¾"	4½"	4½"
1	Harp Support	2"	2"	3½"
2	Plugs	¾"	2"	2"
1	⅛" Std. Pipe			19"
1	⅛" Pipe Hex Nut			
1	Push Thru Brass Socket			
1	9" or 10" Harp to suit shade			
1	Brass Finial			
1	Felt Pad 7" dia.			
4	No. 8 × 1¼" F. H. Wood Screws			
1	Lamp Cord of length to suit			
1	Lamp Shade to suit			
1	Male Plug			

STOCK: White Oak
Important: All dimensions listed below are CUTOUT size.

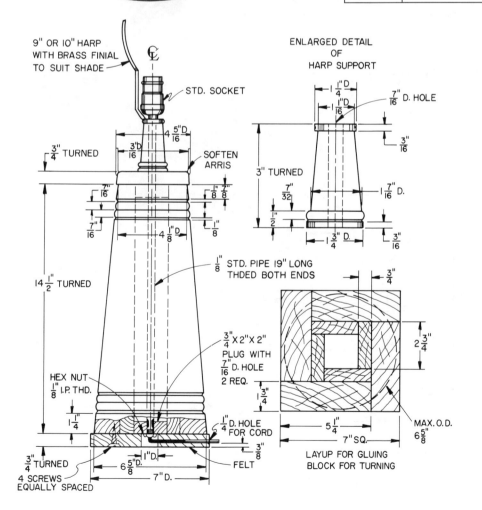

Project 7. Lamp

Bill of Materials

No. of Pieces	Part Name	Thick-ness	Width	Length	Wood
	**Important: All dimensions listed below are FINISHED size.**				
1	Column Cap	1″	4⅛″	4⅛″	Oak
1	Column Base	1¼″	11″	11″	Oak
4	Column Sides	¼″	4″	11″	Weldtex Plywood
1	Corner Block	1″	4⅛″	4⅛″	Oak
4	Corner Glue Strips	⅜″	⅜″	10¼″	White Pine
1	No. 8 IES Shade				
1	2¼ inch Shade Holder				
1	3 way Switch				
1	3 way Bulb				
1	⅛ inch Pipe, 13⅝ inches long, and Nut				
1	Lamp Cord 6 ft. long				
1	14 inch Lamp Shade				

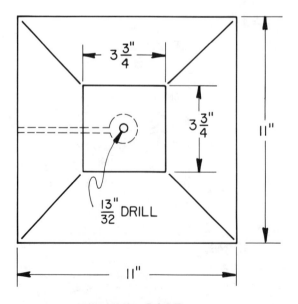

COLUMN BASE

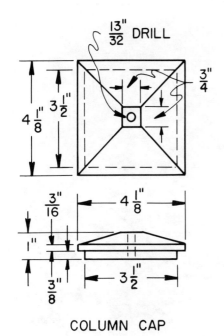

$\frac{13"}{32}$ DRILL

$4\frac{1}{8}"$ $3\frac{1}{2}"$ $\frac{3"}{4}$

$\frac{3"}{16}$ $4\frac{1}{8}"$

$1"$ $3\frac{3"}{8}$ $3\frac{1}{2}"$

COLUMN CAP

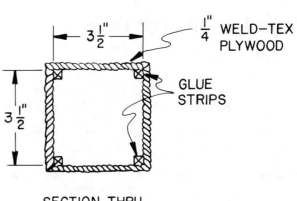

$3\frac{1}{2}"$ $\frac{1"}{4}$ WELD–TEX PLYWOOD

GLUE STRIPS

$3\frac{1}{2}"$

SECTION THRU COLUMN

$4\frac{1}{8}"$

$\frac{13"}{32}$ DRILL

$4\frac{1}{8}"$

$\frac{3"}{16}$

$1"$ $3\frac{1}{2}"$

$\frac{7"}{16}$ $3\frac{3}{4}"$ $\frac{3"}{8}$

COLUMN BLOCK

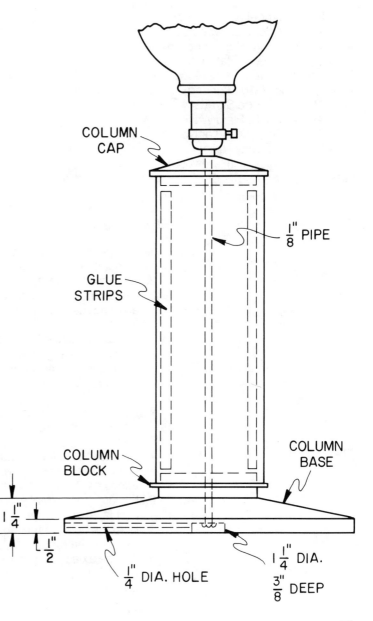

COLUMN CAP

$\frac{1"}{8}$ PIPE

GLUE STRIPS

COLUMN BLOCK

COLUMN BASE

$1\frac{1}{4}"$

$\frac{1"}{2}$

$\frac{1"}{4}$ DIA. HOLE

$1\frac{1}{4}"$ DIA.

$\frac{3"}{8}$ DEEP

Project 8. Outdoor Table

Bill of Materials

No. of Pieces	Part Name	Thick-ness	Width	Length
	STOCK: Redwood or Pine **Important: All dimensions listed below are** FINISHED **size.**			
2	Top	$1^1/4''$	$5^1/2''$	34''
2	Top	$1^1/4''$	$5^1/2''$	32''
2	Top	$1^1/4''$	$5^1/2''$	25''
2	Cleats for Top	$^3/4''$	3''	$29^1/2''$
2	Legs	$1^1/4''$	$2^5/8''$	$20^1/2''$
2	Legs	$1^1/4''$	$2^5/8''$	$26^7/8''$
4	Wheel (Exterior Ply)	$^1/2''$	7''	7''
2	Wheel (Exterior Ply)	$^1/4''$	7''	7''
1	Axle (Hardwood Dowel)	$1^1/2''$		25''
1	Rung (Hardwood Dowel)	$1^1/2''$		20''
28	$1^1/2''$-10 Flathead Wood Screws			
8	$2^1/2''$-10 Flathead Wood Screws			
4	1'' I. D. Plain Washers			
2	Pins (No. 16 or No. 20 Penny Nails)			
2	Wedges (Hardwood)			

Plan of Procedure

1. Cut the pieces for the top $^1/4$ inch longer than the finished length.
2. Cut the cleats for the top.
3. Fasten the top pieces to the cleats, allowing $^3/16$-inch spacing between the top pieces.
4. Lay out the circle for the top, and then take the top apart.
5. Cut the individual top pieces on a band saw and sand on a disc sander.
6. Assemble the top pieces and cleats with waterproof glue and screws.
7. Cut the legs to length, cut angles at the ends, and chamfer the outer edges as shown in the drawing.
8. Lay out the leg joint and cut with a circular saw.
9. Bore the holes in the legs for the axle and the rung.
10. Cut the axle to length, turn ends down to 1-inch diameter on lathe, and drill holes for the pins.
11. Cut the leg rung to length, turn the ends, and make cuts for wedges. Make the wedges from hardwood.
12. Assemble the legs with wedges and glue.
13. Assemble the top and the legs with glue and screws.
14. Cut $7^1/4$-inch wood squares for wheels. Laminate pieces so that center ply grain is at 90-degree angle to grain of outer plies. Use waterproof glue. Cut wheels to size on band saw and sand with disc sander or turn on lathe. Bore 1-inch holes through center.
15. Cut the steel pins to length (16 or 20 penny nails).
16. Sand all surfaces, and apply desired finish.
17. Mount the wheels.

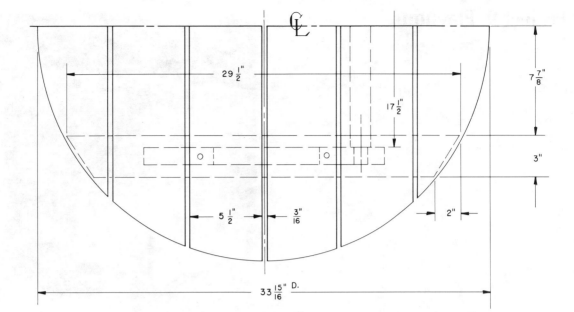

29 ½"

17 ½"

7 ⅞"

3"

5 ½"   3/16"   2"

33 15/16" D.

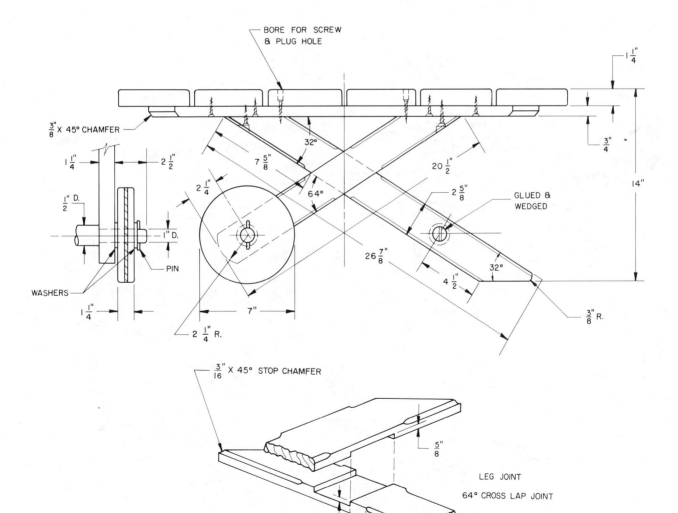

BORE FOR SCREW
& PLUG HOLE

1 ¼"

3/8" X 45° CHAMFER

32°

7 ⅝"

20 ½"

¾"

14"

1 ¼"   2 ½"

½" D.

1" D.

2 ¼"

64°

2 ⅝"

GLUED &
WEDGED

WASHERS

PIN

26 ⅞"

4 ½"

32°

3/8" R.

1 ¼"

7"

2 ¼" R.

3/16" X 45° STOP CHAMFER

5/8"

LEG JOINT

64° CROSS LAP JOINT

5/8"

½"

Project 9. Playhouse

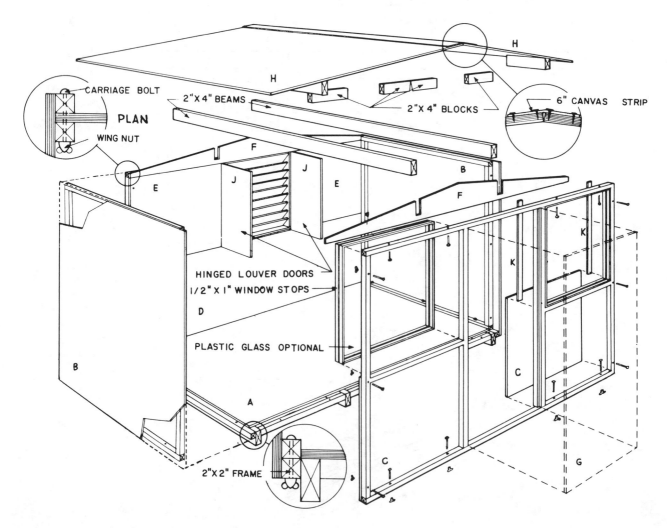

CARRIAGE BOLT

PLAN

WING NUT

2"X 4" BEAMS

2"X 4" BLOCKS

6" CANVAS STRIP

H

H

F

J

J

E

E

B

F

K

K

HINGED LOUVER DOORS

1/2" X I" WINDOW STOPS

D

PLASTIC GLASS OPTIONAL

C

B

A

C

G

2"X 2" FRAME

Bill of Materials

Code	No. Req'd.	Size	Part Identification
A	1	¾″ x 3′-7½″ x 6′-9″	Floor
B	2	½″ x 4′-0″ x 4′-0″	Side
C	2	2′-0″ x 2′-5″	Front Panel
D	1	2′-0″ x 7′-0″	Rear Panel
E	2	1-10⅜″ x 2′-5″	Rear Panel
F	2	7¼″ x 7′-0″	Beam Support
G	1	¾″ x 2′-1⅞″ x 3′-7″	Door
H	2	¾″ x 4′-0″ x 6′-0″	Roof
J	2	1′-10⅜″ x 1′-1″	Louver Door
K	4	1⅝″ x 1′-10⅜″	Casing
	32 Lin. Ft.	2″ x 4″ Stock	Base and Beams
	122 Lin. Ft.	2″ x 2″ Stock	Framing
	50 Lin. Ft.	½″ x 1″ Stock	Stops
	30 Lin. Ft.	½″ x 2½″ Stock	Louvers
	4 Ea. & 2 Ea.	For ½″ x ¾″ Doors	Hinges
	40 Ea.	¼″ Stove	Wing Nuts and Bolts
	2 Pcs.	2′-1¼″ x 1′-10⅜″	Clear Plastic Sheets*
	1 Pc.	6″ x 6′-0″	Canvas Strip

MISCELLANEOUS: 8d common and 6d finishing nails (Galvanized)

No cutting diagram needed for parts "A," "B," "H," "G."

* Optional

Use EXT-APA · A-C plywood only.

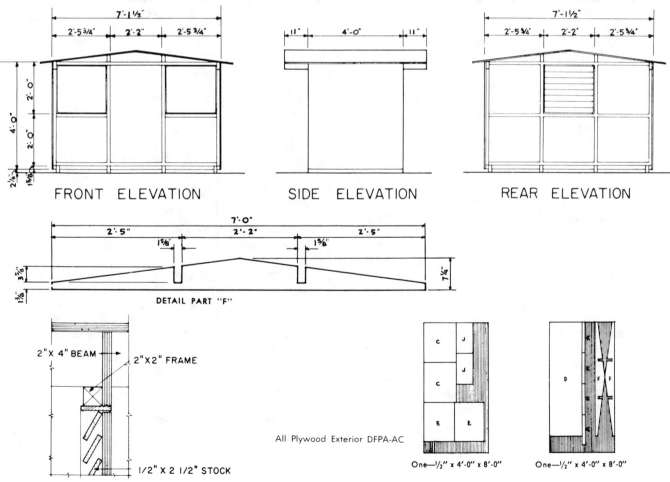

FRONT ELEVATION

SIDE ELEVATION

REAR ELEVATION

DETAIL PART "F"

LOUVER DETAIL

2″ x 4″ BEAM

2″ X 2″ FRAME

½″ x 2 ½″ STOCK

All Plywood Exterior DFPA-AC

One—½″ x 4′-0″ x 8′-0″

One—½″ x 4′-0″ x 8′-0″

Project 10. Mass-Production Project: Book Holder

Plan of Procedure

A. Base			B. Upright		
Operation	**Tools**	**Jigs**	**Operation**	**Tools**	**Jigs**
Rough cut wood to $6^{1}/_{4}$″ x $16^{1}/_{2}$″	C. Saw or radial arm saw		Rough cut wood to 15″ x $5^{1}/_{4}$″	C. saw or radial arm saw	
Joint surface	Jointer		Joint surface	Jointer	
Plane to $^{11}/_{16}$″ thickness	Planer		Plane to $^{5}/_{8}$″ thickness	Planer	
Joint one edge	Jointer		Joint one edge	Jointer	
Square one end	C. Saw or radial arm saw, planer blade		Square one end	C. saw or radial arm saw, planer blade	
Cut to 16″ length	C. Saw or radial arm saw, planer blade		Cut to 7″ length	C. saw or radial arm saw, planer blade	
Cut tapered sides	Circular saw	Taper fixture	Cut a second 7″ length	C. saw or radial arm saw, planer blade	
Joint tapered sides	Jointer		Cut tapered edges	Circular saw	Taper fixture
Rough cut laminate	Circular saw-carbide blade		Joint tapered edges	Jointer	
Apply contact cement to substrate and laminate	Brush, spreader or roller		Rough cut laminate	Circular saw-carbide blade	
Adhere laminate to base	Hand roller		Apply contact cement to both sides of substrate and laminate pieces	Brush, spreader, or roller	
Trim edges of laminate	Router, laminate trimmer				
Round corners of base	Disc sander	Sanding jig	Adhere laminate to both sides of upright	J-Roller	
Hand sand edges of base and bottom surface	150 grit abrasive paper and block		Trim edges of laminate	Router, laminate trimmer, or file	
Drill holes for upright	Drill press	Drill jig	Round corners of base	Disc sander or belt sander	Sanding jig
Stand and seal edges and bottom of substrate to match or complement laminate surface	Penetrating finish		Hand sand edges of upright	150 grit abrasive paper and block	
			Drill anchor holes in upright	Drill press	Drill jig

A. Base			B. Upright		
Operation	Tools	Jigs	Operation	Tools	Jigs
			Stain and seal edges of substrate to match or complement laminate surface	Penetrating finish	
C. Foot			D. Assembly		
Joint one edge of a 1¼″ wide strip	Jointer		Assemble base to upright with 2 1¾″ #10 wood screws	Screwdriver	Assembly fixture
Rip to 1¹/₁₆″ wide	Circular saw		Assemble foot to base 1 1½″ #10 wood screw	Screwdriver	Assembly fixture
Joint to 1″ wide	Jointer				
Cut angle on each piece	Circular saw with miter gauge	Stop block	Polish surface with a soft cloth		
Sand, bevel, and curve	Disc sander or belt sander				
Drill hole	Drill press	Drill jig			
Hand sand all surfaces and edges	150 grit abrasive paper				
Finish with the same stain and sealer used on edges of base and upright	Penetrating finish				

Job Descriptions of the Workers Needed to Mass-Produce the Book Holder

Supervisor—Coordinate all parts of production and make adjustments to keep production going.
Time Keeper—Keep accurate records of the time involved to produce each piece of the final assembly.
Inspectors—Inspect each piece as it is produced for accuracy, finish, etc. Must be able to read measuring devices.
Runners—Convey materials from one work station to another work station.
Circular Saw Operator—Set up and operate circular saw.
Jointer Operator—Operate and adjust jointer.
Glue Person—Spread contact cement evenly and correctly.
Laminate Assembler—Line up materials and adhere them to each other.
Laminate Trimmer—Operate a router or a laminate trimmer.

Disc Sander Operator—Sand edges and curves accurately.
Hand Sanders—Sand a part so it is smooth and scratch free.
Drill Press Operator—Use a drill jig and drill holes accurately as well as setting up the drill press.
Planer Operator—Adjust and operate the planer.
Finishers—Apply finish to edges evenly without finish getting on laminate surface.
Assemblers—Drive screws straight and use an assembly fixture.
Polisher—Wipe off assembled piece so it is ready for distribution.
Radial Arm Saw Operator—Set up radial saw and cross cut pieces to length.
Belt Sander Operator—Sand edges and curves accurately.

(Continued on next page)

Project 10. Mass-Production
Project: Book Holder (Continued)

Bill of Materials

1 piece $^{11}/_{16}$" x 6" x 16" Base—White pine,
fir, popular or other suitable solid wood.
1 piece 6¼" x 16¼" Base Laminate—$^1/_{16}$"
General Purpose Plastic Laminate.
2 pieces 5¼" x 7¼" Upright Laminate—$^1/_{16}$"
General Purpose Plastic Laminate.
1 piece ⅝" x 5" x 7" Upright wood—Same
as is used for base.
1 piece ⅝" x 1" x 3" Foot—Same wood as
is used for base.
2—1¾"—#10 F. H. Steel Wood Screws.
1—1½"—#10 F. H. Steel Wood Screws.
Contact Adhesive.

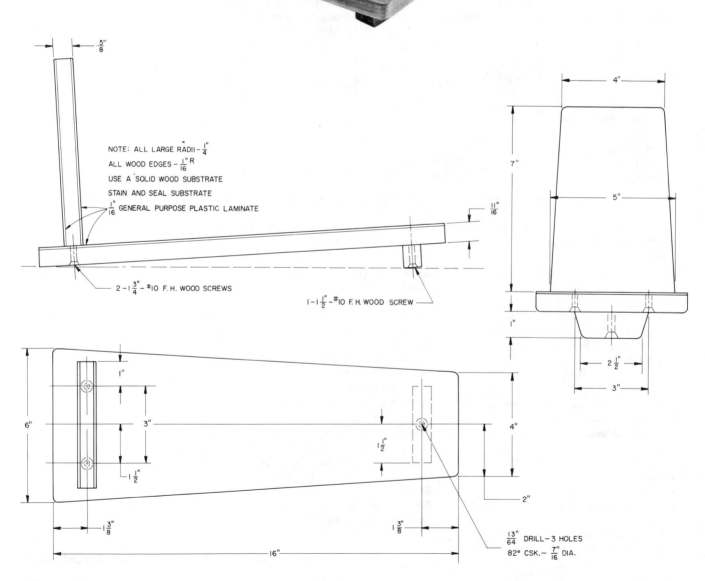

NOTE: ALL LARGE RADII - ¼"

ALL WOOD EDGES - $\frac{1}{16}$" R

USE A SOLID WOOD SUBSTRATE

STAIN AND SEAL SUBSTRATE

$\frac{1}{16}$" GENERAL PURPOSE PLASTIC LAMINATE

2 - 1¾" - #10 F.H. WOOD SCREWS

1 - 1½" - #10 F. H. WOOD SCREW

$\frac{13}{64}$" DRILL - 3 HOLES
82° CSK. - $\frac{7}{16}$" DIA.

Project 11. Cue and Ball Rack

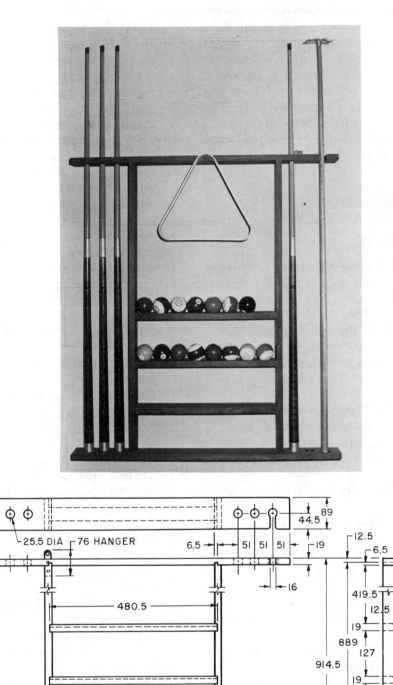

Note: Measurements are in millimetres.

25.5 DIA   76 HANGER   89   44.5   6.5   51 51 51   19   12.5   6.5

480.5   16   419.5   12.5   19   889   127   914.5   19   127   19   127   19

32 DIA   44.5   16   12.5

51 51 51 51   19   468.5   19   51 51 51 51   12.5   12.5   19

204   506.5   204   25.5   38

914.5   89

Reproducibles

This section of the *Instructor's Resource Guide* contains Student Handouts and Student Worksheets that you may duplicate and distribute to the class. The handouts contain information of interest to students. The worksheets require some type of answer or activity. Also included are several Transparency Masters for use with an overhead projector. Following are tips for using each of these reproducibles.

TIPS FOR USING REPRODUCIBLES

STUDENT HANDOUTS

Student Handout 1: A Basic Approach to Solving Problems talks about the steps in problem solving and defines critical thinking.
a) Use during introduction to the course to acquaint students with the thinking skills they'll need to use.
b) Combine with Student Worksheet 1, which suggests a design project that requires problem solving.

Student Handout 2: Plywood—The Versatile Composite gives students background about a product they will be using frequently.
a) Talk about the discussion questions with the class.
b) Show students examples of different kinds of plywood, indicating their uses.

Student Handout 3: Tables 2-A and 2-B are tables from Chapter 2 in the text.
a) Suggest that students keep the handout in a notebook for future reference.
b) Go over the information on the tables to be sure students know how to read it.

Student Handout 4: Table 2-C are tables from Chapter 2 in the text.
a) Suggest that students keep the handout in a notebook for future reference.
b) Go over the information on the table to be sure students know how to read it.
c) Show the class samples of the woods listed.

Student Handout 5: Boosting Your Creativity can be used when covering Chapter 3 on design.
a) Give students 10 minutes to think of as many unusual uses for a brick as they can. Have them read their ideas aloud.
b) Discuss why creativity involves the risk of failure.

Student Handout 6: Customary-Metric Conversions provides a handy reference for converting sizes.
a) Provide the class with at least 10 conversion problems for which they can use the chart.
b) Discuss the advantages of the metric system.

Student Handout 7: General Safety Policies lists safety rules.
a) Discuss the rules with the class, explaining the purpose behind each one.
b) Use in combination with Transparency Master 1 on fire safety.

Student Handout 8: Cordless Portable Tools discusses battery-operated tools, such as drills.
a) Talk about the discussion questions with the class.
b) If battery-operated equipment is available, give a demonstration on its use and care.

Student Handout 9: Table 15-A lists common wood adhesives.
a) Suggest that students keep the handout in a notebook for future reference.
b) Go over the information on the table to be sure students know how to read it.
c) Show students examples of the different adhesives listed.

Student Handout 10: Standard Woodworking Joints lists applications and construction notes.
a) Suggest that students keep the handout in a notebook for future reference.
b) Have students look around the general area for examples of the different joints and identify them.
c) Have students explain how different joints are made.

Student Handout 11: Tables 35-A and 36-A shows common nail and screw sizes.
a) Suggest that students keep the handout in a notebook for future reference.
b) Go over the information on the tables to be sure students know how to read it.

Student Handout 12: Tables 43-A and 43-B shows information on finishes.
a) Suggest that students keep the handout in a notebook for future reference.
b) Go over the information on the tables to be sure students know how to read it.
c) Show the class examples of the different finishes described.

Student Handout 13: Tables 43-C, 43-D, and 43-E shows information on solvents and brushes.

a) Suggest that students keep the handout in a notebook for future reference.

b) Go over the information on the tables to be sure students know how to read it.

c) Show the class examples of the different solvents and brushes described.

Student Handout 14: Engineered Wood discusses the new products being used in construction, such as glulams.

a) Obtain a sample of engineered wood and allow the class to examine it.

b) Talk about the discussion questions.

Student Handout 15: Can We Have Construction Without Destruction? covers how new technologies may help conserve trees.

a) Talk about the discussion questions with the class.

b) Create your own recycling center for lumber in the lab. Encourage students to think of ways to use wood waste products, such as sawdust.

STUDENT WORKSHEETS

Student Worksheet 1: Using Problem Solving to Assist the Handicapped can be used in combination with Student Handout 1, which discusses problem solving and critical thinking.

a) Assign the design project, and display the most inventive results for other classes.

b) Discuss with students the problems handicapped people face when trying to function in a world not designed for their convenience.

Student Worksheet 2: Practice with Fractions is for those students who need remedial work in math.

a) Discuss working with fractions before assigning the worksheet.

b) Ask students to measure a number of objects in the classroom and record the sizes.

Student Worksheet 3: Converting Fractions to Decimals is for those students who need remedial work in math.

a) Discuss the conversion process before assigning the worksheet.

b) Give them a drawing they will use in class and ask them to convert any fractions on it to decimals.

Student Worksheet 4: Hand Tool Identification asks students to write the names of common hand tools.

a) Be sure students have received a demonstration of all these tools.

b) Ask them to write a list of applications for each tool on a separate sheet of paper.

Student Worksheet 5: Job Search Questionnaire acquaints students with using classified ads during a job search.

a) Ask students to draw conclusions from what they have learned during completion of this exercise.

b) Discuss other methods of hunting for a job.

TRANSPARENCY MASTERS

Transparency Master 1: The Correct Choice and Use of Fire Extinguishers lists the types available and tells how to use one.

a) Be sure students know where the fire extinguisher is located in the lab and how to use it.

b) Inform students of specific fire hazards in a woods laboratory.

Transparency Master 2: Measuring in Millimetres shows relative metric sizes.

a) Supply students with metric rulers and ask them to measure a door's thickness, a screw's length, the width of a cabinet knob, and the thickness of a piece of lumber.

b) Ask them to convert the sizes they have recorded to customary sizes.

Transparency Master 3: Computerized Manufacturing shows the different types of manufacturing systems that rely on computers.

a) Show the transparency master when discussing Chapters 1 or 70.

b) Be sure students understand the differences among the different systems.

c) If possible, take the class on a field trip to a plant equipped for computerized manufacturing.

Student Handout 1: A Basic Approach to Solving Problems

Suppose your bedroom closet doesn't have enough room for all of your things. Your parents are nagging you to clean it up, but you realize that won't really solve the underlying problem. Then one day you have an idea. Why not use your woodworking skills to build wooden shelves and partitions that will make better use of the space? It will take some time, but the result will definitely be worth it. Now, all you have to do is figure out how to go about it.

What is the best way to find a solution? Is there a standard process or system you can use? Fortunately, there is. Although there are many different kinds of problems, most of them can be solved using one basic approach. This approach does not always produce the perfect solution. What you are seeking, however, is not perfection. The real goal is to solve a problem to the best of your ability. As you become more skilled at this, your solutions will be that much better.

Finding a solution to the closet problem would proceed like this:

First, recognize the problem and state it clearly. In our example, the problem is the *lack of usable space in the closet.*

Next, research the problem. Try to focus on what will be most helpful. Don't bother to research something with which you are already familiar. Avoid complex data that you don't understand. Perhaps you can find someone who has solved a similar problem. For example, you might visit a store whose specialty is closet organizers. What designs seem to fit your needs?

It is also time to decide on the goals that your solution must fulfill. Ask as many questions as necessary to provide an adequate basis for designing your product. For your organizer you need to know such details as cost, types of materials and tools needed, and how much construction time would be involved.

Next, you can use several methods to decide on possible solutions.

- You can talk the situation over with someone who is not directly involved.
- You can compile a list of all the characteristics of the problem at hand.
- You can use the brainstorming approach in which people share all of their ideas about a problem. For example, you could share ideas with your parents.
- You can sleep on the problem and come back to it with a fresh outlook.

The next step is to eliminate unworkable solutions by evaluating each in terms of the original goals. For example, if you are determined to keep the costs for your closet organizer under $100, you should eliminate any solutions exceeding that cost.

You are now ready to select the best solution, perhaps using models or drawings to assist you in the process. It might even be necessary to reject all the solutions you've considered and start over. Eventually, however, one will seem worthy of a trial.

Finally, your solution must be tested and refined. It is likely that it will need some adjustment. Perhaps, in the case of the closet organizer, it could use a few more shelves. Maybe the organizer makes it difficult to close the closet doors. Continue to test and to modify until you are satisfied.

As you may have noticed as you have been reading, problem solving requires a good deal of critical thinking. Critical thinking is the process of reasonably deciding what to do or believe. From the time you first decide to do something, you are thinking critically. You identify a problem, decide what you want to do, and apply accepted facts and principles. Then you separate the problem into workable parts, combine ideas to create something new, and evaluate your work.

Many problems are solved every day thanks to your problem-solving and critical-thinking abilities. Using the steps outlined in this article can sharpen those abilities.

Discussion Questions

1. Think over the past few days and the problems you solved. Try to remember the steps you took in solving one of them. What were they?
2. What do you think would happen if a person insisted on a *perfect* solution to a problem?

74

Student Handout 2: Plywood—The Versatile Composite

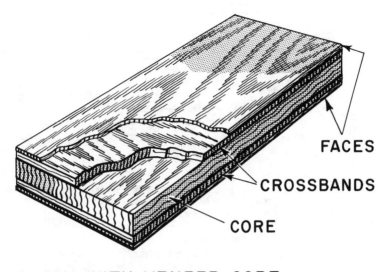

5-PLY WITH VENEER CORE

Plywood is a building material consisting of several thin layers of wood glued together. The layers, referred to as *plies* or *veneers,* are glued so that the grain of each layer is usually at right angles to the grain of the adjacent layers. These alternating layers give plywood greater strength and stability than ordinary wood.

Most plywood has an odd number of plies. The outer plies are called *faces.* In the faces, the grain always runs in the same direction. The center ply is called the core. Any plies between the core and the faces are called *crossbands.* In cases where the plywood has an even number of plies, the grain direction of the two center plies is parallel.

Most plywood is made from softwoods. Only selected logs are used. Plies are cut from the lower portion of the trunk where the wood is mature and strong. Then the wood is placed in dryers where its moisture content is reduced. This provides stability and helps the glue form a tight bond.

Plywood is classified for either interiors or exteriors, depending on the type of glue used. Interior plywood does not require waterproof glue, although it must be able to tolerate occasional moisture. Exterior plywood must always be made with a waterproof glue in order to withstand continued exposure to the weather. It is also cured with heat.

Each plywood sheet is graded according to its strength and appearance. Higher grades are either unblemished or have one flawless face and one face with minor flaws. Better grades are preferred when plywood will be visible in the finished product. Lower grades are used for general construction purposes. An important marking on construction plywood is the span indicator. This tells a carpenter that the plywood can be placed on roof trusses and floor joists up to a certain distance apart.

Plywood is a versatile building material. It can be cut to exact sizes and produced in large panels. Not only does plywood shrink and swell less than ordinary wood, but it also rarely warps and twists. Because it resists splitting at the ends, carpenters can place nails or screws close to its edges.

The principal uses of plywood are for floors, wall paneling, and roof and wall lining. It is also ideal for building the forms used to shape the concrete for buildings and other structures. In addition, plywood appears in a variety of manufactured products, including furniture, boats, and even road signs.

Discussion Questions

1. Name three items that are made at least in part of plywood. Why do you think plywood was used?
2. Why do you think softwoods are used more often to make plywood than hardwoods?

Student Handout 3: Tables 2-A and 2-B (Woods)

Table 2-A. A Guide to Selecting Lumber

Standard Sizes of Softwood			Standard Thickness of Hardwoods		Grade		
						Softwood	Hardwood
Nominal or Stock Size	Actual Size		GREEN Rough	DRIED S2S	1. Yard lumber *Select*—Good appearance and finishing quality. Includes: Grade A—Clear. Grade B—High Quality. Grade C—For best paint finishes. Grade D—Lowest Select.		FAS—Firsts and Seconds. Highest grade.
	Green	Dry					
1″	25/32	3/4″	3/8″	3/16″			No. 1 Common and Select. Some defects.
2″	1 9/16″	1 1/2″	1/2″	5/16″			
3″	2 9/16″	2 1/2″	5/8″	7/16″			
4″	3 9/16″	3 1/2″	3/4″	9/16″	*Common*—General utility. Not of finishing quality. Includes:		No. 2 Common. For small cuttings.
5″	4 5/8″	4 1/2″	4/4 (1″)*	13/16″			
6″	5 5/8″	5 1/2″	5/4 (1 1/4″)	1 1/16″			
7″	6 5/8″	6 1/2″	6/4 (1 1/2″)	1 1/4″	Construction or No. 1—Best Grade. Standard or No. 2—Good Grade. Utility or No. 3—Fair Grade. Economy or No. 4—Poor. No. 5—Lowest.		
8″	7 1/2″	7 1/4″	8/4 (2″)	1 3/4″			
9″	8 1/2″	8 1/4″	12/4 (3″)	2 1/2″			
10″	9 1/2″	9 1/4″	16/4 (4″)	3 1/2″			

Surface	Method of Drying	Method of Cutting	
Rgh. or Rough—as it comes from the sawmill.	AD—Air dried.	Plainsawed or Flat-grained.	2. Shop lumber—For manufacturing purposes. Equal to Grade B Select or better of Yard Lumber. Includes: No. 1—Average 8″ wide. No. 2—Average 7″ wide.
S2S—surfaced on two sides.	KD—Kiln dried.	Quartersawed or Edge-grained.	3. Structural lumber.
S45—surfaced all four sides.			

*Thicknesses are measured in 1/4″ increments for hardwood lumber beginning at 1″. One inch (1″) is called *four quarter*. If you order 4/4 lumber you will receive a board that actually measures 13/16″. If you need a full 1″, then you should order 5/4 lumber.

Table 2-B. A Guide to Selecting Plywood

Hardwoods		Construction and Industrial (Softwoods)	
Grade	Uses	Grade	Uses
Premium grade	Best quality for very high-grade natural finish. Too expensive except for best cabinet work or paneling.	A–A	Best grade for all uses where both sides will show. Exterior or interior.
Good grade (1)	For good natural finish. Excellent for cabinets, built-ins, paneling, and furniture.	A–B	An alternate for A–A grade for high-quality uses where only one side will show. Exterior or interior. The back side is less important.
Sound grade (2)	For simple natural finishes and high-grade painted surfaces.	A–D	A good all-purpose "good-one-side" panel for lesser quality interior work.
Utility grade (3)	Not used for project work.	B–D	Utility grade. Used for backing, cabinet sides, etc.
Reject grade (4)	Not used for project work.		
Widths from 24″ to 48″ in 6″ multiples. Lengths from 36″ to 96″. Veneer-core panels in plies of 3, 5, 7, and 9 are available as follows: 3 ply—1/8″, 3/16″, 1/4″; 5 ply—5/16″, 3/8″, 1/2″ 5 and 7 ply—5/8″; 7 and 9 ply—3/4″. There are three types: Type I is fully waterproof, Type II is water resistant, and Type III is dry bond.		Many other grades for special uses in home construction are available in thicknesses of 1/2″, 3/8″, 5/8″, and 3/4″; both exterior and interior; 1″ is also available in exterior grades. Common widths 3′4″, or 4′; common length is 8′. Be sure to specify exterior grade for outside work (including boats) and interior grade for interior construction.	

Student Handout 4: Table 2-C (Woods)

Table 2-C. Characteristics of Common Woods

Species	Comparative Weights[1]	Color[2]	Hand Tool Working	Nail Ability[3]	Relative Density	General Strength[4]	Resistance to Decay[5]	Wood Finishing[6]
Hardwoods[7]								
Ash, tough white	Heavy	Off-white	Hard	Poor	Hard	Good	Low	Medium
Ash, soft white	Medium	Off-white	Medium	Medium	Medium	Low	Low	Medium
Balsawood	Light	Cream white	Easy	Good	Soft	Low	Low	Poor
Basswood	Light	Cream white	Easy	Good	Soft	Low	Low	Medium
Beech	Heavy	Light brown	Hard	Poor	Hard	Good	Low	Easy
Birch	Heavy	Light brown	Hard	Poor	Hard	Good	Low	Easy
Butternut	Light	Light brown	Easy	Good	Soft	Low	Medium	Medium
Cherry, black	Medium	Med. red-brown	Hard	Poor	Hard	Good	Medium	Easy
Chestnut	Light	Light brown	Medium	Medium	Medium	Medium	High	Poor
Cottonwood	Light	Grayish white	Medium	Good	Soft	Low	Low	Poor
Elm, soft, Northern	Medium	Cream tan	Hard	Good	Medium	Medium	Medium	Medium
Gum, sap	Medium	Tannish white	Medium	Medium	Medium	Medium	Medium	Medium
Hickory, true	Heavy	Reddish tan	Hard	Poor	Hard	Good	Low	Medium
Maghogany, African	Medium	Reddish brown	Easy	Good	Medium	Medium	Medium	Medium
Maghogany, Honduras	Medium	Golden brown	Easy	Good	Medium	Medium	High	Medium
Mahogany, Philippine	Medium	Medium red	Easy	Good	Medium	Medium	High	Medium
Maple, hard	Heavy	Reddish cream	Hard	Poor	Hard	Good	Low	Easy
Maple, soft	Medium	Reddish brown	Hard	Poor	Hard	Good	Low	Easy
Oak, red (average)	Heavy	Flesh brown	Hard	Medium	Hard	Good	Low	Medium
Oak, white (average)	Heavy	Grayish brown	Hard	Medium	Hard	Good	High	Medium
Poplar, yellow	Medium	Lt. to dk. yellow	Easy	Good	Soft	Low	Low	Easy
Walnut, black	Heavy	Dark brown	Medium	Medium	Hard	Good	High	Medium
Willow, black	Light	Medium brown	Easy	Good	Soft	Low	Low	Medium
SOFTWOODS[8]								
Cedar, Tennessee Red	Medium	Red	Medium	Poor	Medium	Medium	High	Easy
Cypress	Medium	Yellow to reddish brown	Medium	Good	Soft	Medium	High	Poor
Fir, Douglas	Medium	Orange-brown	Hard	Medium	Soft	Medium	Medium	Medium
Pine, ponderosa	Light	Orange to reddish brown	Easy	Good	Soft	Low	Low	Medium
Pine, sugar	Light	Creamy brown	Easy	Good	Soft	Low	Medium	Poor
Redwood	Light	Deep red-brown	Easy	Good	Soft	Medium	High	Poor

[1] Kiln-dried weight.
[2] Heartwood. Sap is whitish.
[3] Comparative splitting tendencies.
[4] Combined bending and compressive strength.
[5] No wood will decay unless exposed to moisture. Resistance to decay estimate refers to heartwood only.
[6] Ease of finishing with clear or ''natural'' finishes.
[7] Leaf-bearing tree.
[8] Cone-and-needle-bearing trees.

Student Handout 5: Boosting Your Creativity

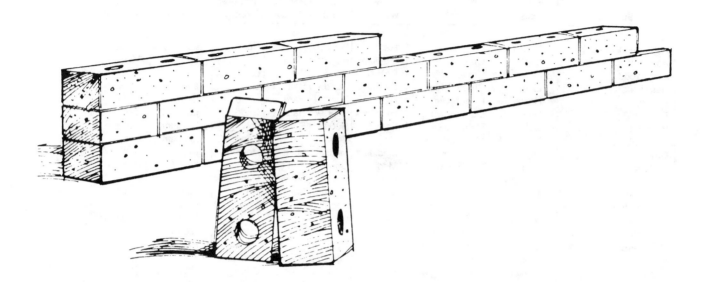

Are you creative? Creative people take bits of experience or information and use it in different combinations to make something new. All people are creative to some extent.

For example, suppose you're locked in a room having one high window. The window is open, but you can't reach it. There are no chairs or ladders in the room, only a shelf filled with books. How would you get out? Did you think of stacking the books on the floor and using them to climb on to reach the window? If so, that was a creative answer. You have used something (the books) in a new way (as a ladder).

Research has shown that there is no link between creativity and superior intelligence. All people can learn to become more creative. Here are some suggestions that may help:

1. Remain open to new ideas. Be willing to experiment, to explore new places, consider new ideas, and meet new people.
2. Commit time and effort to developing new or more advanced skills. Learn about things that interest you. Creativity is fueled by underlying knowledge.

3. Be willing to risk failure. When trying to solve a problem or answer a difficult question, you are likely to make mistakes. Failure teaches you what doesn't work and can lead you to a better answer.
4. Change the way you look at something. For instance, using books to stand on means looking at them as something besides reading material. Loosen up.
5. Try to put yourself in someone else's place. If you're a young man, pretend for a minute that you're a young woman. If you're tall, pretend that you're very short. How does the world look to you from a different viewpoint?
6. You are what you think you are. If you think you're creative, you will be.

One well-known test for creativity involves thinking of uses for a brick. Some uses are obvious, such as a doorstop or a paperweight. However, all the uses do not have to be serious. For example, with snow packed on it, a brick might make a ski slope for mice. Take ten minutes now and think of as many uses for a brick as you can. Write them down. You'll be surprised at how many you can think of!

Student Handout 6: Customary-Metric Conversions

Use this handy chart for reference when converting to metric sizes.

Customary (English)	METRIC				
	Actual	Accurate Woodworkers' Language	Tool Sizes	Lumber Sizes	
				Thickness	Width
1/32 in	0.8 mm	1 mm bare			
1/16 in	1.6 mm	1.5 mm			
1/8 in	3.2 mm	3 mm full	3 mm		
3/16 in	4.8 mm	5 mm bare	5 mm		
1/4 in	6.4 mm	6.5 mm	6 mm		
5/16 in	7.9 mm	8 mm bare	8 mm		
3/8 in	9.5 mm	9.5 mm	10 mm		
7/16 in	11.1 mm	11 mm full	11 mm		
1/2 in	12.7 mm	12.5 mm full	13 mm	12 mm	
9/16 in	14.3 mm	14.5 mm bare	14 mm		
5/8 in	15.9 mm	16 mm bare	16 mm	16 mm	
11/16 in	17.5 mm	17.5 mm	17 mm		
3/4 in	19.1 mm	19 mm full	19 mm	19 mm	
13/16 in	20.6 mm	20.5 mm	21 mm		
7/8 in	22.2 mm	22 mm full	22 mm	22 mm	
15/16 in	23.8 mm	24 mm bare	24 mm		
1 in	25.4 mm	25.5 mm	25 mm	25 mm	
1 1/4 in	31.8 mm	32 mm bare	32 mm	32 mm	
1 3/8 in	34.9 mm	35 mm bare	36 mm	36 mm	
1 1/2 in	38.1 mm	38 mm full	38 mm	38 mm	
1 3/4 in	44.5 mm	44.5 mm	44 mm	44 mm	
2 in	50.8 mm	51 mm bare	50 mm	50 mm	50 mm
2 1/2 in	63.5 mm	63.5 mm	63 mm	63 mm	
3 in	76.2 mm	76 mm full		75 mm	75 mm
4 in	101.6 mm	101.5 mm		100 mm	100 mm
5 in	127.0 mm	127 mm			125 mm
6 in	152.4 mm	152.5 mm			150 mm
7 in	177.8 mm	178 mm bare			
8 in	203.2 mm	203 mm full			200 mm
9 in	228.6 mm	228.5 mm			
10 in	254.0 mm	254 mm			250 mm
11 in	279.4 mm	279.5 mm			
12 in	304.8 mm	305 mm bare			300 mm
18 in	457.2 mm	457 mm full	460 mm		
24 in	609.6 mm	609.5 mm			
36 in	914.4 mm	914.5 mm			
48 in—4'	1219.2 mm	1220 mm			
96 in—8'	2438.4 mm	2440 mm			

Panel Stock Sizes

1220 mm width
2440 mm length

Customary length, in feet	6	8	10	12	14	16	18	20
Replacement length, in metres	1.8	2.4	3.0	3.6	4.2	4.8	5.5	6.0

Student Handout 7: General Safety Policies

Learn these rules. Know why they're important. Obey them at all times.

1. All students must wear clothing suitable to the activity (lab coats, aprons, or school clothes).

2. Remove or securely fasten neckties, jewelry, loose clothing, long hair, etc.

3. Students must wear approved safety eye protection at all times while in a laboratory, except in safe areas as designated by the instructor.

4. All guards and other safety equipment must be in place and operating correctly.

5. Students must have permission from the instructor at all times to work in the laboratory.

6. Know where and how to find first aid.

7. Don't leave a running machine unattended.

8. Accident reports must be filled out on *all injuries* and *near injuries.*

9. All material and equipment damage must be reported.

10. All guards provided by the manufacturer must be in place and used.

11. No student may use any machine on which he/she has not been properly instructed.

12. There must be at least two people present in a laboratory when power equipment is used.

13. Keep the area and work surfaces clean of scraps, liquids, and unnecessary equipment.

14. No horseplay or roughhousing is allowed in the laboratory.

Student Handout 8: Cordless Portable Tools

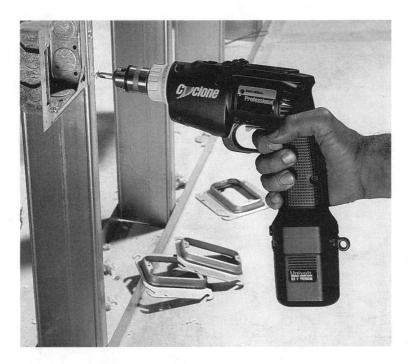

Many manufacturers now offer portable tools powered by nickel-cadmium batteries. The most popular seems to be the battery-operated drill. Such drills are very useful where electrical power is not available or where long extension cords could not be used.

The battery for a cordless drill is contained in its handle in a plastic battery pack. When the battery runs low, it can be detached from the drill and placed in a battery charger. The charger is then plugged into a regular wall outlet. The battery regains full power in approximately one hour.

Discussion Questions

1. In what types of construction projects might such a drill be most useful?
2. What other kinds of tools might benefit from battery power? Why? What tools might *not* make good choices for battery power? Why?
3. What disadvantages might there be to using battery-powered equipment?

Student Handout 9: Table 15-A (Adhesives)

Table 15-A. Wood Adhesives

Type	Description	Recommended Use	Care in Using	Correct Use
Hide glue	Comes in flakes to be heated in water or in prepared form as liquid hide glue. Very strong, tough, light color.	Excellent for furniture and cabinetwork. Gives strength even to joints that do not fit very well.	Not waterproof; do not use for outdoor furniture or anything exposed to weather or dampness.	Apply glue in warm room to both surfaces and let it become tacky before joining. Clamp 3 hours.
Casein	From milk curd. Comes in powdered form. Must be mixed with water.	For inside and woodwork. Almost waterproof. Good for oily woods. Inexpensive. Good for heavy wood gluing.	Some types require bleaching. Will deteriorate when exposed to mold.	Mix with water to creamy consistency. For oily woods, sponge surfaces with dilute caustic soda one hour before gluing. Apply with brush. Clamp and allow to dry for three hours at 70 degrees.
Urea-resin adhesive	Comes as powder to be mixed with water and used within 4 hours. Light colored. Very strong if joint fits well.	Good for general wood gluing. First choice for work that must stand some exposure to dampness, since it is almost waterproof.	Needs well-fitted joints, tight clamping, and room temperature 70° or warmer.	Make sure joint fits tightly. Mix glue and apply thin coat. Allow 16 hours drying time. Dries in seconds with electronic gluer.
Resorcinol (waterproof)	Comes as powder plus liquid; must be mixed each time used. Dark colored, very strong, completely waterproof.	This is the glue to use with exterior type plywood for work to be exposed to extreme dampness.	Expense, trouble to mix, and dark color make it unsuitable to jobs where waterproof glue is not required.	Use within 8 hours after mixing. Work at temperature above 70°. Apply thin coat to both surfaces. Allow 16 hours drying time.
Liquid resin (white) polyvinyl glue	Comes ready to use at any temperature. Clean working, quick setting. Strong enough for most work, though not quite as tough as hide glue.	Good for indoor furniture and cabinetwork. First choice for small jobs where right clamping or good fit may be difficult.	Not sufficiently resistant to moisture for outdoor furniture or outdoor storage units.	Use at any temperature but preferably above 60°. Spread on both surfaces, clamp at once. Sets in 1½ hours.
Contact cement	Comes in a can as a light tan liquid.	Excellent for bonding veneer plastic laminates, leather, plastics, metal foil, or canvas to wood.	Adheres immediately on contact. Parts can't be shifted once contact is made. Position accurately. Temperature for working must be 70° F or above.	Stir cement. Apply two coats to both surfaces. Brush on a liberal coat. Let dry for 30 minutes. Apply second coat. Allow to dry for not less than 30 minutes. Test for dryness by pressing wrapping paper to surface. If paper doesn't stick, the surfaces are dry and ready for bonding.
Epoxy cement	Comes in two tubes, or cans, that must be mixed in exact proportions.	Excellent for attaching hardware and metal fittings to wood. Good for extremely difficult gluing jobs. Will fill large holes.	Epoxies harden quickly. Mix only what can be used in half hour. Use at temperatures above 60 degrees. Keep epoxy compounds separate. Don't reverse caps.	Mix small amounts. Clean and roughen the surfaces. Remove oil, dirt, and other loose matter. Apply to surfaces with putty knife. Clean tools immediately. Press parts together.
Hot-melt glues	Cream colored polyethylene based adhesive in stick form.	Quick bonding adhesive; best for small areas.	Glue hardens quickly. Work fast before glue cools.	Apply small amounts. Don't spread. Press surfaces together for 20 seconds.

82

Student Handout 10: Standard Woodworking Joints

Use this handy chart for reference when making design decisions.

	APPLICATIONS	CONSTRUCTION NOTES	SIMILAR TYPES	
Edge Butt	Building larger surfaces for table tops, desks and other furniture.	Make a spring type joint with circular saw and jointer. Use drill press for dowel joint. Fasten by gluing.	Dowel, Spline, Rabbet. All used to strengthen the adjoining surfaces.	**Dowel** **Spline** **Rabbet**
Corner Butt	For simple box construction, cases, inexpensive drawers, millwork, frame structures, chairs.	Keep corner square by using miter gauge on saw. Assemble with nails or screws and/or glue. Use doweling jig and drill press for doweled corner.	Glued and Blocked. Used for greater strength. Doweled Corner, a substitute for mortise and tenon.	**Glued and Blocked** **Dowel**
Dado	Use it in shelves, steps, drawers, bookcases.	Cut with dado head on circular saw. Fit piece into dado. Assemble with glue.	Blind Dado (gain) for high quality furniture.	**Blind Dado (Gain)**
Rabbet	Corners of modern furniture, simple drawer construction.	Cut rabbet on circular saw, band saw or shaper. Depth of rabbet, about two thirds the thickness of the stock. Glue, nail or assemble with long screws.	Dado and Rabbet. For better drawer construction.	**Dado and Rabbet**
Miter	Picture frames, boxes, modern furniture molding, etc.	Use miter gauge and cut on circular saw or band saw. Fit corner carefully. Assemble with glue or nails.	Dowel, Spline. Both for strengthening adjoining surfaces.	**Dowel** **Spline**
Cross Lap	Furniture construction, doors, frames, stretchers for tables and stands.	Lay out carefully. Cut with dado head. Make press fit. Assemble with glue.	End Lap for frames. Middle Lap for doors.	**Middle Lap** **End Lap**
Thru Multiple Dovetail	Fine box and drawer construction.	Lay out dovetail carefully. Cut on jig saw or shaper. Assemble with glue.	Secret Dovetail for high quality furniture. Lap Dovetail for better drawer construction.	**Secret Dovetail** **Lap Dovetail**
Blind Mortise and Tenon	Tables, chairs and other pieces on which rails are fastened to legs.	Cut tenon on circular saw using dado head if one is available. Cut mortise on drill press with mortising attachment. Fit accurately. Glue for permanency.	Open Mortise and Tenon for frame work. Haunched Mortise and Tenon for panel construction. Keyed Mortise and Tenon for mission furniture.	**Open Mortise and Tenon** **Keyed Mortise and Tenon** **Haunched Mortise and Tenon**

Student Handout 11: Tables 35-A and 36-A (Fasteners)

Table 35-A. Nail Sizes

Penny Number	Length in Inches	Number Per Pound		
		Common Nails	Box Nails	Finishing Nails
2	1	876	1010	1351
3	1¼	568	635	807
4	1½	316	437	548
6	2	181	236	309
8	2½	106	145	189
10	3	69	94	121
12	3¼	64	87	113
16	3½	49	71	90
20	4	31	52	62
30	4¾	20		
40	5			
50	5½			
60	6			

Table 36-A. Common Wood Screw Sizes

The bottom part of the table shows the correct size of drills and/or auger bits needed to install the screws.

Length	Number of Screw Size																	
¼ inch	0	1	2	3														
⅜ inch			2	3	4	5	6	7										
½ inch			2	3	4	5	6	7	8									
⅝ inch				3	4	5	6	7	8	9	10							
¾ inch					4	5	6	7	8	9	10	11						
⅞ inch							6	7	8	9	10	11	12					
1 inch							6	7	8	9	10	11	12	14				
1¼ inch								7	8	9	10	11	12	14	16			
1½ inch							6	7	8	9	10	11	12	14	16	18		
1¾ inch									8	9	10	11	12	14	16	18	20	
2 inch									8	9	10	11	12	14	16	18	20	
2¼ inch										9	10	11	12	14	16	18	20	
2½ inch													12	14	16	18	20	
2¾ inch														14	16	18	20	
3 inch															16	18	20	
3½ inch																18	20	24
4 inch																18	20	24
Diameter In Inches At Body	.060	.073	.086	.099	.112	.125	.138	.151	.164	.177	.190	.203	.216	.242	.268	.294	.320	.372
Shank Hole Hard & Soft Wood	1/16	5/64	3/32	7/64	7/64	1/8	9/64	5/32	11/64	3/16	3/16	13/64	7/32	1/4	17/64	19/64	21/64	3/8
Pilot Hole Soft Wood	1/64	1/32	1/32	3/64	3/64	1/16	1/16	1/16	5/64	5/64	3/32	3/32	7/64	7/64	9/64	9/64	11/64	3/16
Pilot Hole Hard Wood	1/32	1/32	3/64	1/16	1/16	5/64	5/64	3/32	3/32	7/64	7/64	1/8	1/8	9/64	5/32	3/16	13/64	7/32

Student Handout 12: Tables 43-A and 43-B (Finishing)

Table 43-A. Wood Finishing Characteristics

Name	Relative Hardness[1]	Grain	Finish
Ash	Hard	Open[2]	Requires filler.
Basswood	Soft	Close[3]	Paints well.
Beech	Hard	Close	Poor for paint, takes varnish well.
Birch	Hard	Close	Stains and varnishes well.
Cedar	Soft	Close	Paints well. Finishes well with varnish.
Cherry	Hard	Close	Requires filler.
Fir	Soft	Close	Can be painted, stained, or finished natural.
Gum	Soft	Close	Can be finished with variety of finishes.
Mahogany	Hard	Open	Requires filler.
Maple	Hard	Close	Takes any type finish.
Oak	Hard	Open	Requires filler.
Pine	Soft	Close	Takes any type finish.
Walnut	Hard	Open	Requires filler. Takes all finishes well.

Notes: [1]"Hard" and "soft" refer to the relative hardness of wood; no relation to hardwoods or softwoods.
[2]"Open grain" is associated with varying pore sizes between springwood and summerwood.
[3]"Close grain" is associated with woods having overall uniform pore sizes.

Table 43-B. Finishes

Finish (solvent)	Application	Drying Time	Durability	Color	Appearance	Notes
Wax (none)	Hand rub with soft cloth.	30 minutes	Good moisture resistance.	Tends to yellow with age.	Soft sheen	Paste wax can be used for sealer.
Shellac (alcohol)	Wide brush or hand wipe.	30-60 minutes	Poor. Water turns shellac white. No outdoor use.	Orange shellac dries honey-colored. White shellac dries clear.	Sheen to gloss	Good as a liquid wood filler on some woods. Better as a sealer.
Oil: Boiled Linseed (turpentine or mineral spirits)	Rub with soft cloth.	Indefinite	Will not peel or crack.	Darkens quickly.	Soft sheen	Driers can be added to increase hardness.
Oils: Sealacell, Watco, Tung (mineral spirits)	Rub with soft cloth.	2 days	Will not peel or crack. Better moisture resistance.	Dull, but shines to satin luster when steel wool is used between coats.	Soft sheen	Finish is more durable than boiled linseed oil.
Varnish (turpentine or mineral spirits)	Bristle brush or foam polybrush.	1-1½ days	Good weather and wear resistance.	Spar varnish tends to darken.	Sheen to gloss	Avoid shaking varnish. Apply several thin coats. Finish in dust-free place.
Lacquer brushing (lacquer thinner)	Brush (sable or camel).	4 hours	Fair moisture resistance, good durability.	Will not discolor wood.	High gloss	Foam polybrush can be used.
Lacquer spraying (Lacquer thinner)	Spray.	Dries quickly.	High durability.	Clear. Slight yellowing with age.	Gloss. Can be steel-wooled to soften sheen.	Use spray booth.
Enamels and paints (turpentine or water)	Brush or pad.	2-4 hours	Closs is very durable. Can be washed.	Any color or tint.	Opaque. Covers surface completely.	Adds beauty to soft woods.

Student Handout 13: Tables 43-C, 43-D, and 43-E (Finishing)

Table 43-C. Selecting the Proper Brush for the Job

Size	Application
1″ to 1½″	Touch-ups and little jobs, such as toys, tools, furniture legs, and hard-to-reach corners.
2″ to 3″	Trim work, such as sashes, frames, molding, or other flat surfaces. An angular-cut brush helps do clean, neat, sash or narrow trim work and makes edge cutting easier.
3½″ to 4″	For large flat surfaces, such as floors, walls, or ceilings.
4½″ to 6″	Large flat areas, particularly masonry surfaces, barns, or board fences.

Table 43-D. Solvents to Be Used with Certain Finishing Materials

Solvent	Finishing Material
Turpentine	Oil stain Filler for varnish and shellac finish Varnish Enamel
Turpentine and linseed oil	Paint
Alcohol	Shellac
Lacquer thinner	Filler for lacquer finish Lacquer

Table 43-E. Characteristics of Solvents

Kind	Flammable	Source	Uses	Comments
Turpentine	Yes	Sap of pine trees.	Thinning oil and alkyd-base paints. Cleaning brushes. A final finish on certain woods.	Costly. Strong odor.
Mineral spirits	Yes	Refined petroleum product.	Thinner for oil and alkyd paints and varnish. Cleaning brushes.	Cannot be used to clean hardened paint brushes.
Naphtha (Benzene)	Highly	From coal tar.	Thinning oil-based paints. Removing spots.	Makes paint dry very fast. Wear gloves and mask when using.
Denatured alcohol (Ethyl)	Highly	From wood drippings and chemicals.	Thins shellac. Cleans shellac brushes.	Softens shellac. Dangerous to drink. Affects certain finishes.
Acetone	Highly	From various alcohols and acetic acid.	Paint, varnish, and lacquer removers.	Attacks all finishes. Wear gloves and mask.

Student Handout 14: Engineered Wood

New ideas in the construction industry sometimes take hold slowly. Materials and techniques must have a proven track record. In recent years, the industry has accepted two new products:

- *Laminated-veneer lumber* (including I-beams)
- *Glue-laminated beams,* or *glulams*

Laminated-veneer lumber (LVL) is made with wood veneer. Douglas fir and Southern yellow pine are most commonly used. Sheets of veneer are dried to a uniform moisture content in large open-ended ovens. Each sheet is graded and checked for quality.

Next, the veneer is fed through an automatic glue-spreader. Each sheet is coated with a layer of adhesive. The adhesive is waterproof, heat resistant, and very strong. The glued sheets are assembled with the highest-grade veneers on the top and bottom to improve the overall strength of the finished product. Then the sheets are fed into a machine that cures the adhesive using heat and pressure.

The laminated I-beam or I-joist is used in floor construction as a joist or in place of rafters in roof construction. I-beams have several advantages over solid lumber. They are available in 60-foot or longer lengths, so a single I-beam can span the entire width of a house. A wood I-beam is lighter than an equal length of solid lumber, making it easier to handle and install. Installation is faster and requires fewer workers.

Laminated-veneer headers and beams can be used in place of solid wood or built-up headers. This product consists of many layers of veneer laminated together into a solid material with a rectangular cross-section. Many builders believe that the nail-holding ability of LVL headers and beams is considerably greater than that of solid lumber.

Glue-laminated beams (glulams) are used in place of steel or solid lumber to span great distances. Garage door headers and structural stair stringers are examples. They are also used for open floorplans having large rooms.

Glulam beams are made by laminating lengths of dimension lumber using structural adhesives. The individual layers of the beam are adhered face to face, clamped together, and allowed to cure at room temperature. Southern yellow pine and Douglas fir are also used to make glulams. The strength and rigidity of the resulting material are greater than that of solid timber of equal dimensions.

Engineered wood products like LVL and glulams enable builders to support longer spans than would be possible with conventional lumber. In the past steel or solid timber supports were required. However, traditional wood framing methods and connectors can still be used. The innovation of engineered wood has given builders a greater range of choices.

Discussion Questions

1. Why do you think new ideas take hold slowly in the construction industry?
2. In what ways does laminated-veneer lumber resemble plywood?

Student Handout 15: Can We Have Construction without Destruction?

Harvesting wood can be harmful to the environment. A tree's roots act as natural anchors, holding soil in place. Without trees, precious soils are blown or washed away, making the land unsuitable for growing other types of vegetation. Trees supply oxygen and they provide shelter and food for animals. Though the harvested trees are often replaced with new trees or other vegetation, these are often not native to that area. In addition, it takes many years for trees to grow. All of this upsets the ecosystem of an area. *Ecosystems* are the interdependent plant and animal communities found in nature. Deserts and jungles are examples of ecosystems.

With new technology, houses can now be built out of recycled materials. A company in British Columbia has glued, pressed, and then microwaved strips of scrap wood to produce a wood similar to new wood. New types of cement made from scrap stone, wood, and plastic are available. A company in Illinois makes nails by melting down scrap metal.

Another way of recycling is re-using. Millions of board feet of lumber from houses that have been torn down get tossed into landfills. Much of this wood is still good, but building codes require that lumber have a grade stamp. Codes need to be changed so old wood may be evaluated and given a stamp of approval, too.

Discussion Questions

1. Are there any companies in your area that salvage old building materials? Find out more about them.
2. What problems do you think might arise when evaluating old wood?

Student Worksheet 1: Using Problem Solving to Assist the Handicapped

No one can do everything. Disabilities exist in different forms and in varying degrees of seriousness in all people. Serious disabilities, such as not being able to walk, are often referred to as handicaps. Today, advances in technology are freeing more and more people from limitations resulting from physical handicaps. Devices can be developed to enable people with handicaps to perform tasks they would ordinarily find difficult or be unable to do.

For this activity you will design a computer work station for a handicapped person. The problem solving process will be essential. Keep the various steps of that process in mind as you work on this project. (See *Student Handout 1: A Basic Approach to Solving Problems*) Because the final product will be constructed of wood, you will be drawing upon information you have learned in class. Your invention can be:

- intended to aid any type of physical handicap.
- a modification of an existing work station.
- a totally new concept.

Specifications

Your work station design will need to meet certain standards. Read the following specifications carefully before you begin.

Your work station design must:
- help a person with a physical handicap.
- be safe.
- be supported in writing with a written description and drawings.
- be explained in a presentation to the class that describes how the work station would operate and how it would assist the specific handicap.

Materials

pencils and paper
computer and CAD software (optional)

Procedure

1. Your teacher will divide the class into teams.
2. Both your idea and how you develop it will be up to you. Still, certain steps will make your work easier. Keeping the problem-solving process in mind, some of these steps might be helpful.
   - Brainstorm with your design team and evaluate your proposals.
   - Draw rough sketches of promising ideas.
   - Interview someone with a physical handicap to share ideas.
   - Gather needed materials and tools.
   - Create technical drawings of the work station.
3. Using this list as a guideline, include any other steps that you feel are necessary.

Evaluate

When you've completed your work station design, evaluate it. Discuss it with your teacher and classmates. Among the factors to consider are usefulness, safety, innovativeness, and cost-effectiveness.

Student Worksheet 2: Practice with Fractions

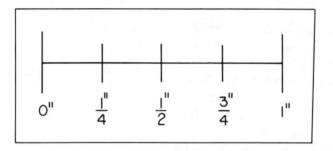

You will need a ruler, paper and pencil, and colored pencils.

1. Draw a four-inch line at the top of your paper with a regular pencil. Make the end points (vertical lines) one-inch high and label them "0" and "1," as shown in the drawing.

2. Using a red pencil, divide this line into four equal parts and label them as shown. Use shorter vertical lines than you did for the end points and make these red lines all the same height. These segments represent *fourths*.

3. Using your blue pencil, divide each fourth of your line in half. Use shorter lines to mark these new segments and make the blue lines all the same height. These segments represent *eighths*.

4. Using your green pencil, divide each eighth of your line in half, using even shorter vertical lines to mark the new segments. Make all the green lines the same height. The new segments are *sixteenths*.

5. Count all the lines on your drawing between the 0 and the 1. Each of these lines is what fraction of an inch?

_____

6. What fraction of an inch does each blue line represent?

_____

7. What fraction of an inch does each red line represent?

_____

8. Find the ⁵/₈″ mark and label it.

9. Find the ¹¹/₁₆″ mark and label it.

10. Find the ¼″ mark and label it.

11. What do you think is the purpose of making the vertical lines different heights?

_____

_____

_____

Student Worksheet 3: Converting Fractions to Decimals

Decimal = Fraction

1.00	=	1″						
.50	=	$^1/_2$″	=	$^2/_4$″	=	$^4/_8$″	=	$^8/_{16}$″
.25	=	$^1/_4$″	=	$^2/_8$″	=	$^4/_{16}$″		
.125	=	$^1/_8$″	=	$^2/_{16}$″				
.0625	=	$^1/_{16}$″						

1. Refer to the Decimal = Fraction chart. Note that $^1/_8$″ is equal to .125. If you want to convert $^5/_8$″ to a decimal, how would you do it?

   _____

   _____

   _____

2. Find $^5/_8$″ on the drawing of the ruler and label it.

3. Convert $^7/_{16}$″ to a decimal.

   _____

4. Find $1^7/_{16}$″ on the ruler and label it.

5. Add $^3/_8$ to $^1/_8$. Find the result and label it.

6. Subtract $^5/_{16}$ from $^7/_{16}$.

   _____

7. Change $^1/_4$ and $^1/_{16}$ to decimals; then add them.

   _____

8. You can convert any fraction to a decimal by dividing the numerator (upper part) by the denominator (lower part). Using this method, convert $^3/_4$ to a decimal.

   _____

9. If a dollar equals 1.00

   ● what is the decimal equivalent of a half-dollar? _____

   ● what is the decimal equivalent of a quarter? _____

   ● what is the decimal equivalent of a dime? _____

   ● what is the decimal equivalent of a nickel? _____

   ● what is the decimal equivalent of a penny? _____

Student Worksheet 4: Hand Tool Identification

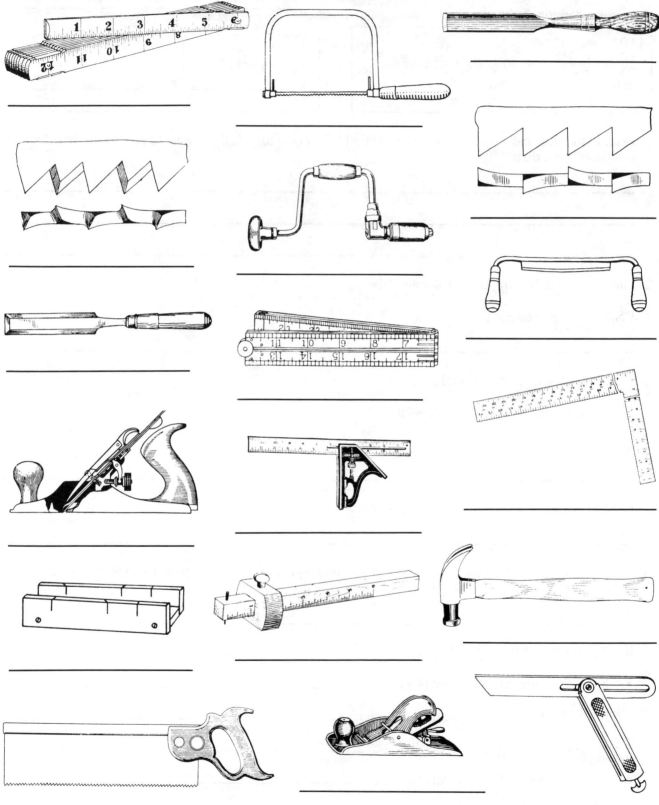

Name _____ Class _____ Date _____

Student Worksheet 5: Job Search Questionnaire

Directions: Obtain 3 different newspapers and review the job ads. Look for jobs related to industrial technology.

1. On the lines below, write the names of the newspapers you looked through.

Newspaper A _____

Newspaper B _____

Newspaper C _____

2. Choose two ads for jobs that interest you. Read the ads carefully, and then fill in the following information about the two jobs. If the information is not given in the ad, write NA (for "Not Available") in the blank.

	Ad 1	Ad 2
Position title	_____	_____
Location of job	_____	_____
Education or degree needed	_____	_____
Experience needed	_____	_____
Date position is available	_____	_____
Work hours	_____	_____
Salary	_____	_____
Person to contact	_____	_____
Phone and/or address	_____	_____

3. Was it easy for you to decide on the two jobs you chose from the classified ads? _____

4. About how many ads for industrial-related jobs did you find in:

Newspaper A? _____

Newspaper B? _____

Newspaper C? _____

5. In a few complete sentences, describe your reaction to the number and types of jobs advertised in the classified ads you read.

Transparency Master 1:
The Correct Choice and Use of Fire Extinguishers

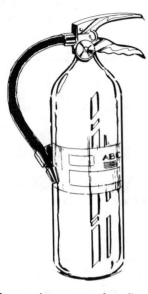

1. The main parts of a fire extinguisher: the trigger, safety ring, and baton.

2. Holding the fire extinguisher firmly, pull out the safety ring.

3. Pick up the extinguisher with one hand on the trigger. Use the other hand to aim the baton at the base of the fire. Squeeze the trigger to spray the extinguisher. Continue spraying until the fire is completely out.

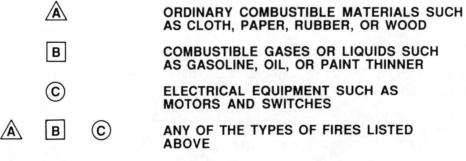

CLASS	TYPE OF FIRE
Ⓐ	ORDINARY COMBUSTIBLE MATERIALS SUCH AS CLOTH, PAPER, RUBBER, OR WOOD
Ⓑ	COMBUSTIBLE GASES OR LIQUIDS SUCH AS GASOLINE, OIL, OR PAINT THINNER
Ⓒ	ELECTRICAL EQUIPMENT SUCH AS MOTORS AND SWITCHES
Ⓐ Ⓑ Ⓒ	ANY OF THE TYPES OF FIRES LISTED ABOVE

Transparency Master 2: Metric Measurement

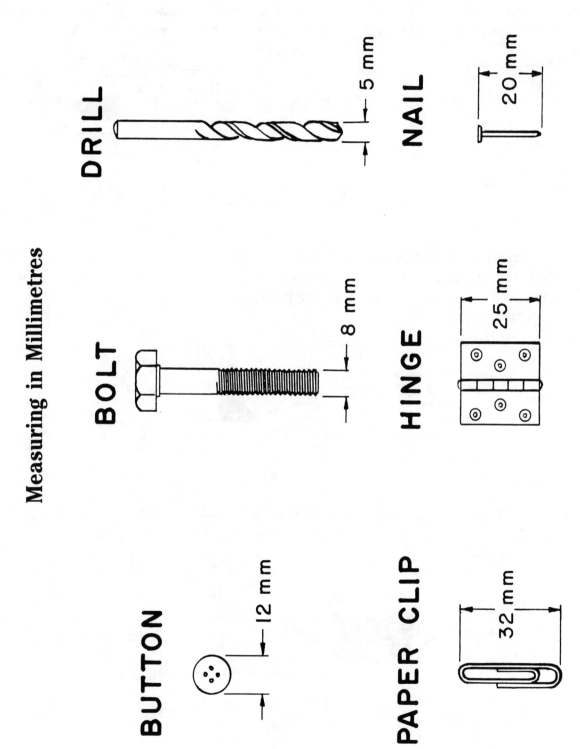

Measuring in Millimetres

DRILL — 5 mm

NAIL — 20 mm

BOLT — 8 mm

HINGE — 25 mm

BUTTON — 12 mm

PAPER CLIP — 32 mm

Transparency Master 3: Computerized Manufacturing

1. Computer-Aided Design (CAD)
Designers use computers to do their drawings.

2. Computer-Numerical-Control (CNC)
Computers tell machines how to process a part.

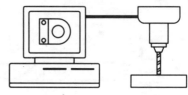

3. Computer-Aided Manufacturing (CAM)
A design made on one computer is sent to another computer, which then instructs a machine how to make the item.

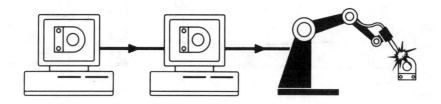

4. Computer-Integrated Manufacturing (CIM)
All areas of manufacturing are linked by a mainframe computer.

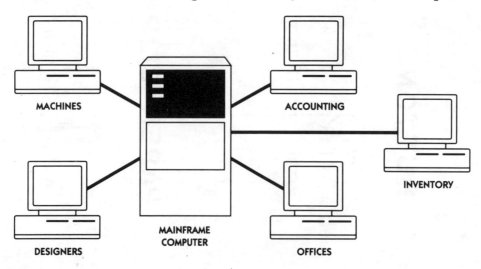